# Contents

# Chapter 1
# Introduction to Databases

## What is Microsoft Access?

Microsoft Access is one of the most widely used database packages. Databases are used to store large amounts of information, and allow you to sort and filter the information or data to provide useful reports.

A database is based on tables of data, and each table contains many records (rows).

A record consists of many fields.

This is an example of a table of data:

**Tip:**

In this book, we will look at databases containing just one table, but it is possible for databases to contain many tables.

| Field Name | Bird Name | Date First Spotted | Where Spotted |
|------------|-----------|--------------------|---------------|
| Field Contents | Barn Owl | 01/01/2001 | Hutton Heath |
| | Pigeon | 01/01/2001 | Town Square |
| | Duck | 03/01/2001 | Park Lake |
| | Common Sparrow | 15/02/2001 | Back Garden |

*Table 1.1*

? How many rows are there in the table?

? How many columns are there in the table?

? How many fields are there in each record?

A There are 4 rows. Each row holds one record, so there are 4 records in this table.

A There are 3 columns. The column headings are the field names.

A There are 3 fields in each record – the same as the number of columns.

The bird watcher can use the database to find out information such as:

▶ Whether or not he has spotted a particular bird

▶ Which birds he has spotted on Hutton Heath

▶ In which location had he spotted the most birds for the first time

▶ What date he first spotted a particular bird

▶ How many birds he spotted for the first time in January 2001

Databases are not often used for such small amounts of data, because the answers to the above questions can be easily answered just by looking at the table. However, if you had spotted hundreds of birds there would be hundreds of rows, and the table would be so big it would take hours to answer the questions. This is where a database becomes very useful.

Before creating a database on the computer it is important to plan your database.

# Planning a database

When planning a database you need to think about:

**?** What is the purpose of the database?

**?** What information will you want to look up in the database?

**?** What data will you store in the database?

# Activities Database

You are going to design a database for a local youth club that is planning various activity weekends for its members.

**Purpose of the database:**

The leader of the youth club needs be able to find out quickly and easily:

**?** Who's going on a particular activity (for a register);

**?** How many of the people signed up for a particular activity want transport (so transport can be arranged);

**?** Contact name and number of a particular member.

After talking to the leader of the youth club, you have found out:

- The youth club is planning 4 activity weekends.

- Each weekend will involve a different activity, either abseiling, canoeing, horse riding or archery.

- The weekends each cost £20 in total.

- The youth club will provide optional transport from the headquarters to wherever the activity is taking place.

- The youth club needs to have a contact name (e.g. parent's name) and telephone number for each member.

Your database should contain details about each member and their chosen activity. The next step is to decide which fields to have in your table. Based on the information given above, the table must contain the following information about each member:

- Name

- Date of birth

- Contact name

- Contact number

- Chosen activity

- Amount paid

- Transport required?

This list will be used to decide what fields are needed in your table.

**Tip:**
Remember that the fields in the table are the column headings.

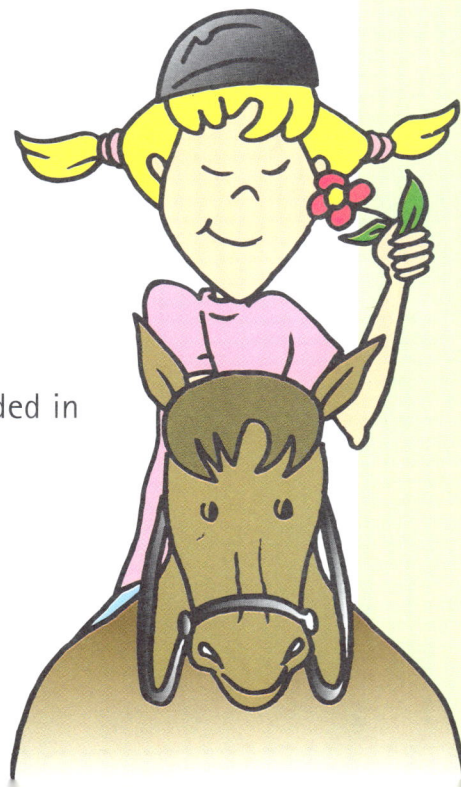

# Data Types

Before you can enter these fields into your database, you need to think about what format the data will be in. Access has many different data types, which are explained in the table below:

| | |
|---|---|
| Text | Letters, symbols and numbers, i.e. Alphanumeric data. |
| Number | Numbers only (no letters). Includes numbers with decimal points. |
| Date/Time | Dates and times. |
| Currency | For all monetary data. Access will insert a currency symbol before the amount (such as £ or $, etc.) |
| Yes/No | Used wherever the field can only take 2 values, Y/N, True/False etc. |
| AutoNumber | This is a unique value generated by Access for each record. |

*Table 1.2*

# Deciding on data types

You will have to choose a data type for each field from the table given above. For example, should you hold a telephone number as a Text field or a Number field? At first you may think that a Number field would be best but in practice this is a bad idea for two reasons:

Access will not record leading zeroes in a number field. So if the telephone number is 0149450 it will be recorded as 149450 which is incorrect.

Access will not allow you to put a space, bracket or hyphen in a number field. So you will not be able to record a telephone number as, for example, 01473 874512.

# Selecting fields

We already have a list that will form the basis of the fields in the database (Name, DateOfBirth). You may now wish to split some of the pieces of information, for example, Name will include a *first name* and a *surname*. Should you split this into two fields? There are two main reasons why you may wish to do this:

- If you want to sort the members alphabetically by surname, this is much easier to do if surname is a separate field.

- You may wish to search for a particular member record. It will be much easier to search on the surname.

# Designing the database structure

The structure of the database can be thought of as what the table will look like without any information in (the design of the table). To describe the structure you need to know:

- The number of fields (columns) in the table

- The field names (column headings)

- The data type of each field

The number of rows will change as the user enters more data, and is not part of the database structure.

It is important to know the difference between the database structure (think of the empty table) and the data held in the database (the information that you put into the table).

For each of the following changes to the Bird database, would you need to change the database structure or edit the data?

**?** You decide to add a new field name, Weather, to the database.

**?** The pigeon was actually spotted in the park, not the town square.

**A** If you add a new field name, you are changing the database structure.

**A** If you are changing the pigeon record, you are only editing the data.

# Naming conventions

We will use a common name notation when naming tables and field names. This means putting tbl in front of the table names, and not using any spaces in any of the names. Use capital letters in the middle of a field name to make the words easier to read. Look at the table below to see an example.

Information about the database structure can be shown in a table, such as the one shown below:

tblMember

| Field Name | Data Type |
|------------|-----------|
| MemberNo | AutoNumber |
| FirstName | Text |
| Surname | Text |
| ContactName | Text |
| ContactNo | Text |
| DateOfBirth | Date/Time |
| Activity | Text |
| AmountPaid | Currency |
| Transport? | Y/N |

*Table 1.3*

This will be the database structure of the Activities database.

**Tip:**
You can use letters, numbers, spaces and special characters like ?, &. Don't use an exclamation mark (!) or a full stop in a field name.

# *Chapter 2*
# *Creating a New Database*

Over the next several chapters you'll be creating and developing the Activities database.

## Loading Access

You can load Access in one of two ways:

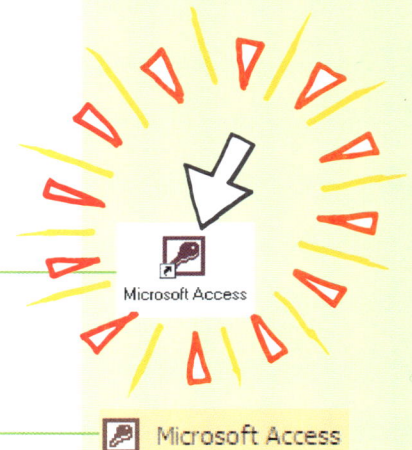

- Either double-click the Access icon on the main screen in Windows

- or click the Start button at the bottom left of the screen, then click Programs, then click Microsoft Access.

Your screen will look like Figure 2.1a if you are using Access 2000 or Figure 2.1b if you are using Access 2002:

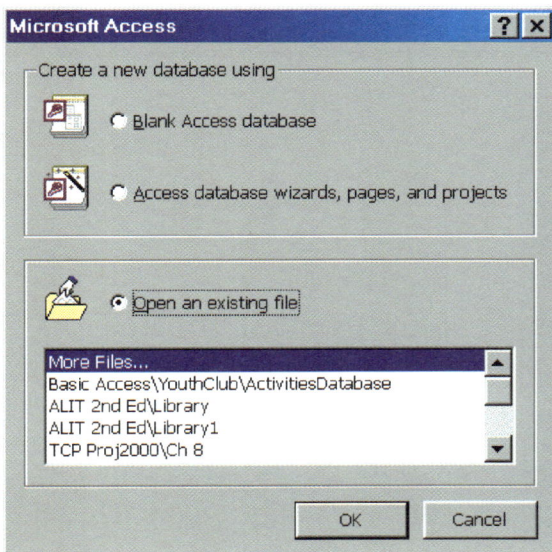

Figure 2.1a

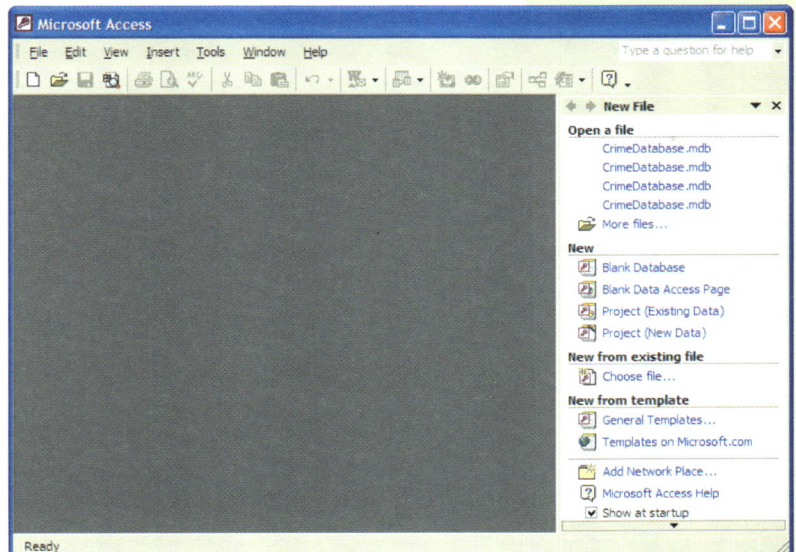

Figure 2.1b

You now have the option of either opening an existing database or creating a new one. We will create a new database from scratch.

▶ In Access 2000 select the Blank Access Database button and press OK. In Access 2002 click the blue Blank Database option in the right hand pane.

A window opens as shown below, asking you to select a folder and a name for your new database.

▶ Click the Create New Folder button and create a new folder named YouthClub.

▶ In the File Name box, type the name ActivitiesDatabase (no spaces), and press the Create button. Access will automatically add the file extension .mdb.

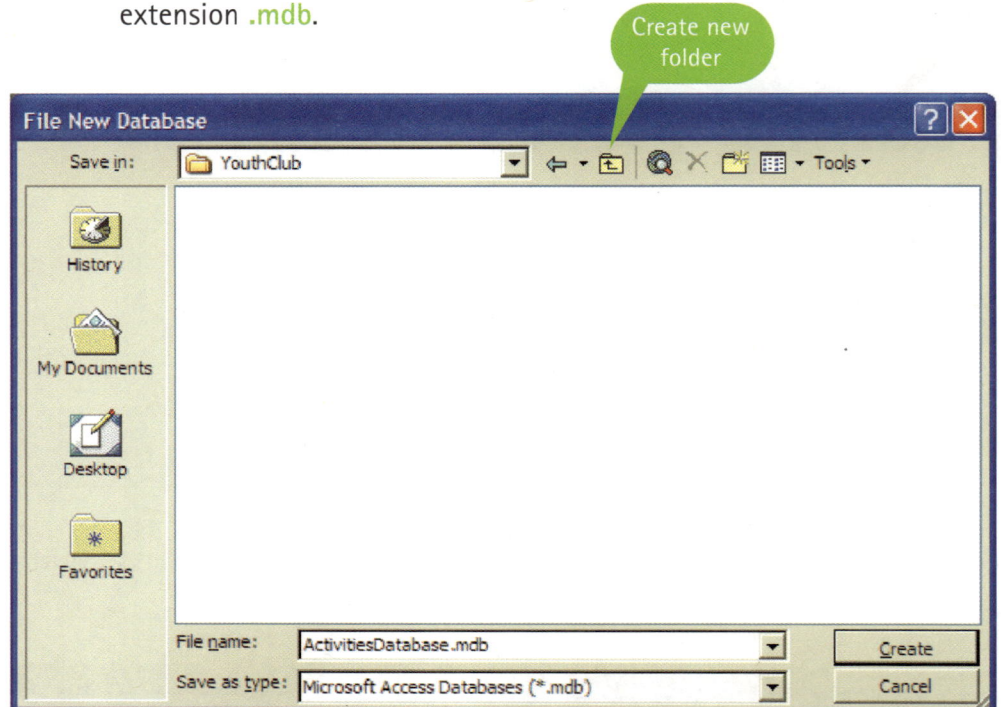

Figure 2.2: Saving a new database

# The database structure

The first thing you have to do is set up the database structure. As you learnt in the first chapter, all data in an Access database is stored in tables. A table has a row for each record and a column for each field. The first thing you have to do is tell Access exactly what fields you want in each record, and what data type each field is. After this has been done and the structure is saved, you can start adding data to the database.

# The Database window

Access databases are made up of objects. A table is an object, and is the only object we have talked about so far. Other objects which you will come across in this book include Queries, Forms and Reports.

Every Access Database has a Database window. This is a sort of central menu for your database, from which you can open the objects in your database. The window has buttons (or tabs in Access 7 and 97) for each type of database object (Tables, Queries, Forms, Reports, etc.).

Tables is currently selected, and since at the moment there are no existing tables to Open or Design, only the Create options are active.

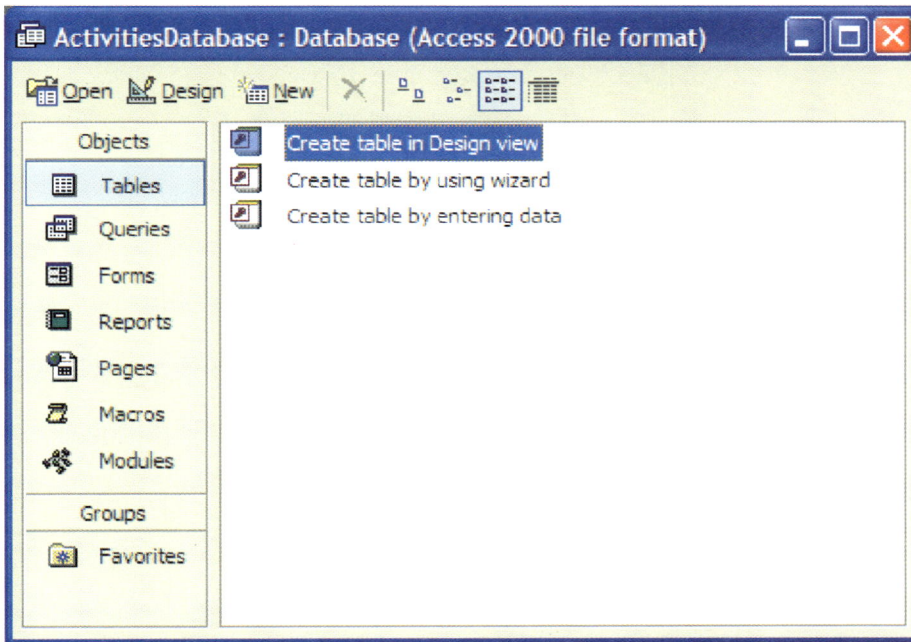

*Figure 2.3: The Database window*

**Note:**

Access will automatically choose Access 2000 file format. This means you can open your database in both Access 2002 and Access 2000.

11

# Creating a new table

**New**

▶ In the Database window make sure the Tables tab is selected, and press New.

A New Table window appears as shown below.

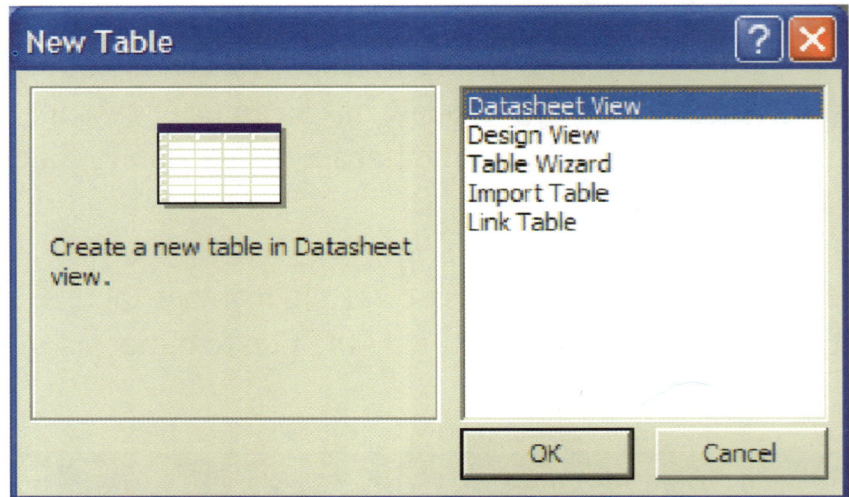

*Figure 2.4: Creating a new table*

▶ Select Design View and click OK.

The Table Design window appears.

Look back at the structure of the tblMember table in Table 1.3. All these fields need to be entered in the new table.

▶ Enter the first field name, MemberNo, and tab to the Data Type column.

▶ Click the Down arrow and select the field type AutoNumber.

▶ Tab to the Description column and type This is the Key field.

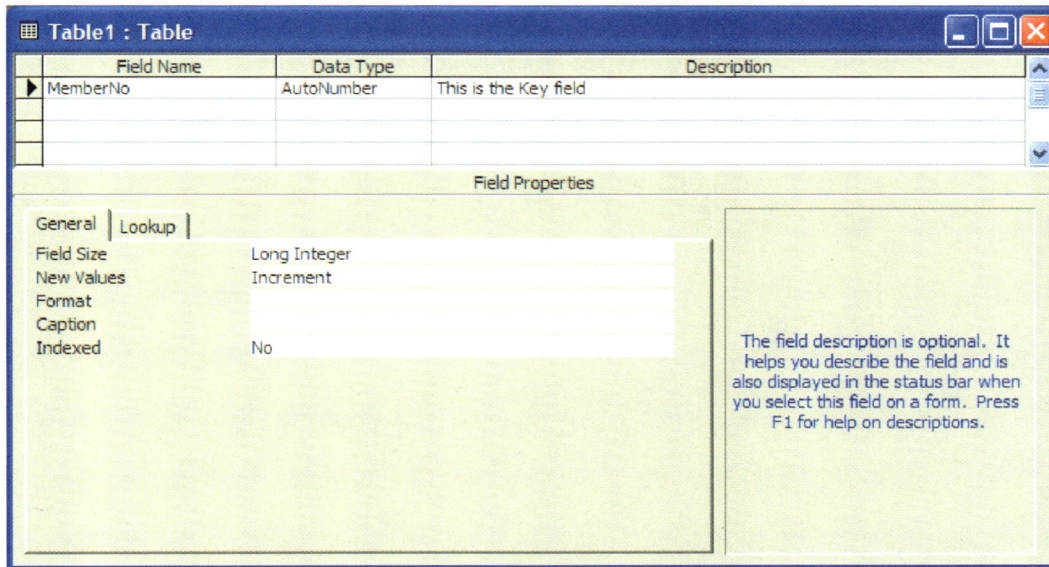

| Field Name | Data Type | Description |
|---|---|---|
| MemberNo | AutoNumber | This is the Key field |

Field Properties

General | Lookup

| | |
|---|---|
| Field Size | Long Integer |
| New Values | Increment |
| Format | |
| Caption | |
| Indexed | No |

The field description is optional. It helps you describe the field and is also displayed in the status bar when you select this field on a form. Press F1 for help on descriptions.

*Figure 2.5: Entering field names*

# Defining the primary key

Every table in an Access database must have a primary key (also known as the key field). The field which you specify for the primary key must have a different value for each record. For the Activities database we will set MemberNo to be the primary key. We cannot use Surname because there may be more than one member with the same surname.

▶ With the cursor still in the row for MemberNo, press the Primary Key icon on the toolbar. The key symbol appears in the left hand margin next to MemberNo.

# Entering other fields

Now we can enter all the other fields.

▶ In the next row, enter the field name FirstName and leave the data type in the next column as Text.

▶ Enter the fields for Surname, ContactName and ContactNo. All these fields have a data type Text.

▶ Enter the field name DateOfBirth and give it a data type of Date/Time.

▶ Enter the field name Activity and leave the data type as Text.

▶ Enter the field name AmountPaid and give it the data type Currency.

▶ Enter the field name Transport? and give it the data type Yes/No.

Your table should now look like Figure 2.6.

**Tip:**

Don't worry if you make a few mistakes – after all the fields are entered, you will learn how to move fields around, delete them or insert new fields. You can correct any mistakes at that point and it will be good practice.

Row selector

| | Field Name | Data Type | Description |
|---|---|---|---|
| 🔑 | MemberNo | AutoNumber | This is the Key field |
| | FirstName | Text | |
| | Surname | Text | |
| | ContactName | Text | |
| | ContactNo | Text | |
| | DateOfBirth | Date/Time | |
| | Activity | Text | |
| | AmountPaid | Currency | |
| ▶ | Transport? | Yes/No | |

**Table1 : Table**

**Field Properties**

General | Lookup

| | |
|---|---|
| Format | Yes/No |
| Caption | |
| Default Value | |
| Validation Rule | |
| Validation Text | |
| Required | No |
| Indexed | No |

The data type determines the kind of values that users can store in the field. Press F1 for help on data types.

*Figure 2.6: The table structure*

# Saving the table structure

▶ Save the table structure by pressing the Save icon or selecting File, Save from the menu bar. Don't worry if you've made some mistakes in the table structure – they can be corrected in a minute.

▶ You will be asked to type a name for your table. Type the name tblMember and click OK.

▶ Click the Close icon in the top right-hand corner to close the window. You will be returned to the Database window.

# Editing a table structure

▶ In the Database window you will see that your new table is now listed.

> **Tip:**
> If you have named the table wrongly, or made a spelling mistake, right-click the name and select **Rename**. Then type in the correct name.

▶ Select the table name tblMember, click the Design View icon and you are returned to Design View.

# Inserting a field

To insert a new row for a second contact number (maybe for a work phone number) just above Activity:

▶ Click the row selector (left hand margin) for Activity.

▶ Press the Insert key on the keyboard or click the Insert Rows icon on the toolbar.

▶ Enter the new field name ContactWorkNumber, data type Text.

# Deleting a field

Now, to delete the field you have just inserted:

▶ Select the field by clicking the row selector for ContactWorkNumber.

▶ Press the Delete key on the keyboard or click the Delete Rows icon on the toolbar.

If you make a mistake, you can use Edit, Undo Delete from the top menu bar to restore the field.

# Moving a field

▶ Click the row selector to the left of the field's name to select the field.

▶ Click again and drag to where you want the field to be. You will see a line appear between fields as you drag over them to indicate where the field will be placed.

Tip:
The row selector is the square to the left of the field name.

# Changing or removing a key field

▶ To change the key field to Surname, click the row selector for the Surname field and then click the Primary Key icon on the toolbar.

▶ To remove the primary key altogether, select the row that is currently the key field and click the Primary Key icon on the toolbar.

When you have finished experimenting, restore MemberNo as the key field of this table. Make any other necessary corrections to leave the fields as specified in Figure 2.6, and save the table structure.

▶ Save and close your database by selecting File, Close from the menu bar and saving changes when prompted.

# Chapter **3**
# Datasheet View

## Opening an existing database

▶ Load Access. One of the following windows will appear. Your screen will look like Figure 3.1a if you are using Access 2000 or Figure 3.1b if you are using Access 2002:

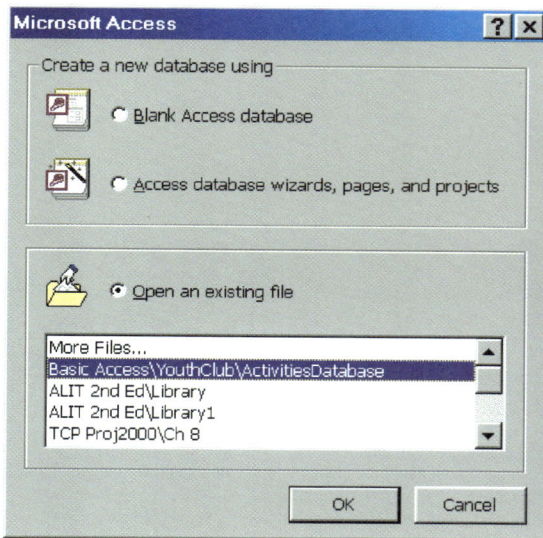

Figure 3.1a: Opening an existing database

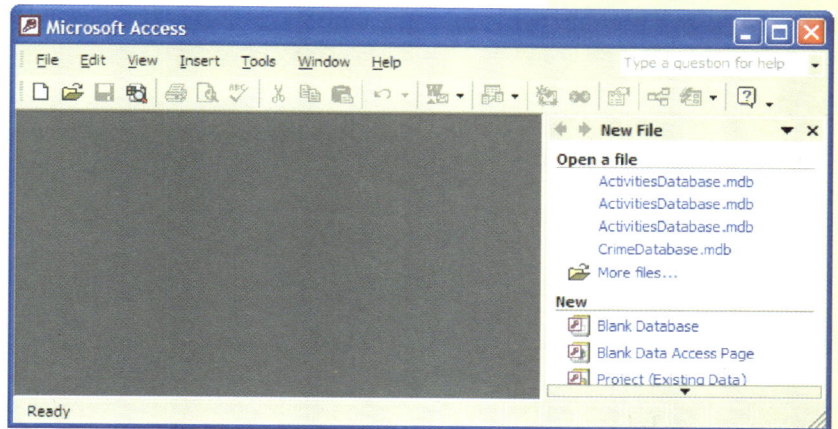

Figure 3.1b: Access 2002

▶ In Access 2000 select Open an existing file, then find the file ActivitiesDatabase in the box below. It should be in a folder named YouthClub. In Access 2002, select ActivitiesDatabase from the list on the right.

▶ Click OK.

The Database window will appear.

# Table Views

There are two 'views' to choose from when making changes to your database:

*i* **Design View** is used for making changes to the database **structure**, for example adding a field or changing a field name. This is the view that you used in the last chapter to set up the database structure of the **Activities** database.

*i* **Datasheet View** is used for entering and editing the data held in the database. In this chapter we will be using **Datasheet View** to enter information about the members into the **tblMember** table.

# Entering Data

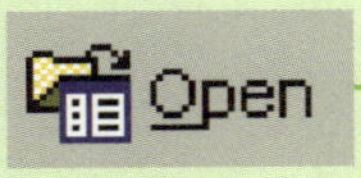

▶ With **tblMember** selected, click the **Open** button in the Database window.

The table now appears in **Datasheet View** as shown below.

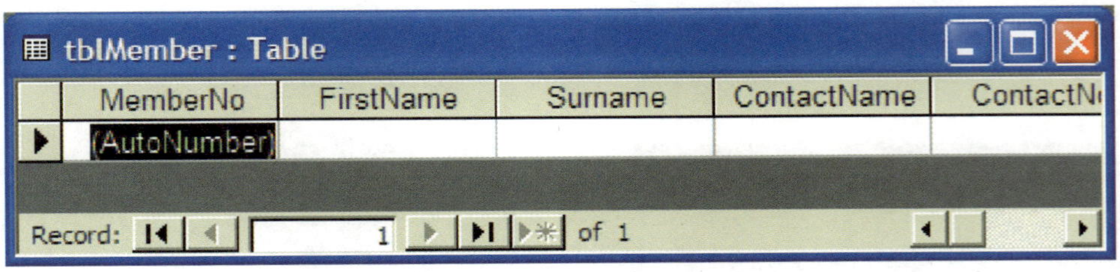

| | MemberNo | FirstName | Surname | ContactName | ContactN |
|---|---|---|---|---|---|
| ▶ | (AutoNumber) | | | | |

Record: ◀◀ ◀ 1 ▶ ▶◀ ▶* of 1

*Figure 3.2: Empty table in Datasheet View*

You can drag the right border of any column header (field name) to alter its width. Drag the borders so that the whole row appears on the screen.

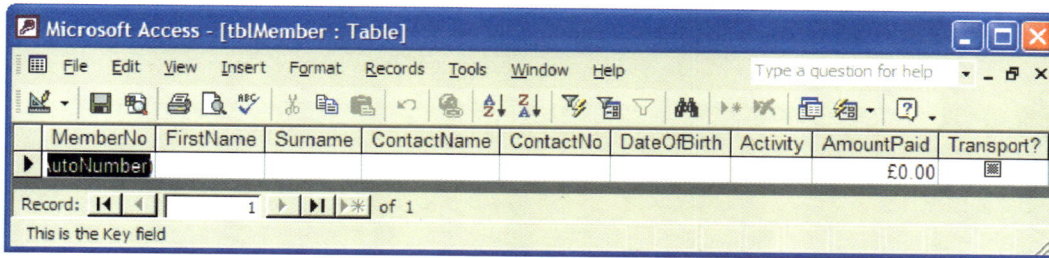

**Microsoft Access - [tblMember : Table]**

File Edit View Insert Format Records Tools Window Help    Type a question for help

| MemberNo | FirstName | Surname | ContactName | ContactNo | DateOfBirth | Activity | AmountPaid | Transport? |
|---|---|---|---|---|---|---|---|---|
| AutoNumber | | | | | | | £0.00 | ☒ |

Record: ◄ ◄    1  ► ►► ►* of 1

This is the Key field

*Figure 3.3: Adjusted column widths*

Click in the first row of the MemberNo column, where it says (AutoNumber). Access will automatically put a value in here, so you don't have to enter anything.

Press the Tab key to move to the next field, or just click in the next field with the mouse.

Enter the name John.

Go to the Surname field and type Hainsworth.

Go to the ContactName field and type Mrs Hainsworth.

Go to ContactNo and type 01474 678456.

Go to DateOfBirth and enter 26/5/89.

Enter Windsurf as the activity.

Leave AmountPaid as 0.00. You do not need to type the £ sign, Access adds it automatically because you have specified the Currency field type.

In the Transport? field, either click in the check box or press the Spacebar to put a tick in it.

Tip:
Double-click the right-hand border of a column header to automatically resize it.

Your table should now look like the one below:

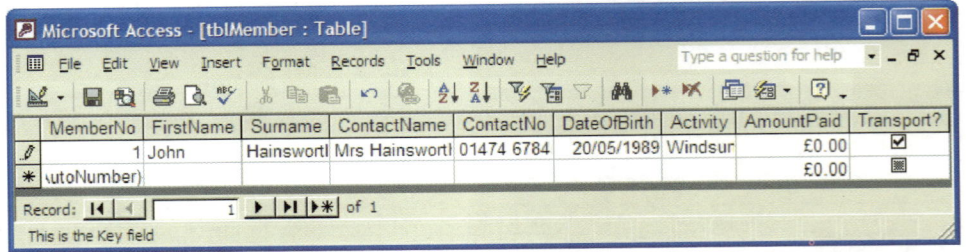

*Figure 3.4*

Now enter the rest of the data from the table shown below.
Remember that MemberNo will be added automatically by Access.

| FirstName | Surname | ContactName | ContactNo | DateOfBirth | Activity | Amount Paid | Transport? |
|-----------|---------|-------------|-----------|-------------|----------|-------------|------------|
| John | Hainsworth | Mrs Hainsworth | 01474 678456 | 26/5/89 | Windsurf | £0 | Y |
| Tony | Hodson | Mr Hodson | 01474 212394 | 7/9/84 | Abseil | £15 | Y |
| Mike | Stevenson | Mr Denton | 01474 665498 | 15/11/90 | Abseil | £20 | N |
| Sharron | Hart | Mr Hart | 01474 374509 | 22/4/85 | Riding | £10 | Y |
| Richard | Ellis | Mrs Muller | 01474 151884 | 12/8/88 | Windsurf | £20 | N |
| Lucie | Harris | Mrs Harris | 01474 908635 | 14/12/90 | Riding | £20 | Y |

*Table 3.5*

*Fee was all for combining some of her activities, Robin was not so sure.*

When you have entered all the data, click the Close icon in the top right hand corner of the current window. (Be careful to close just the table window, not Access.)

▶ If you have changed the column widths, you will be asked if you want to save the changes you made to the layout.

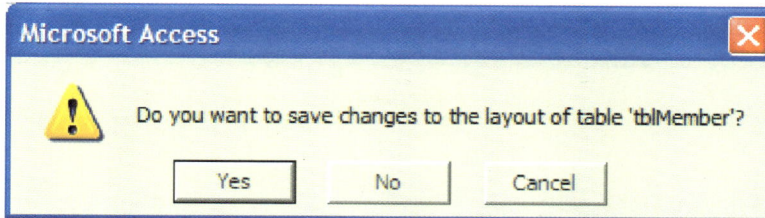

**Microsoft Access**

⚠ Do you want to save changes to the layout of table 'tblMember'?

[ Yes ]     [ No ]     [ Cancel ]

▶ Click Yes. You will be returned to the Database window.

# Finding, editing and deleting data in a table

▶ In the Database window, make sure that Tables is selected in the list of objects on the left of the window.

▶ Select tblMember and click Open. This will open the table in Datasheet View. (If you wanted to change the actual structure of the table, for example to add a new field, you would select Design.)

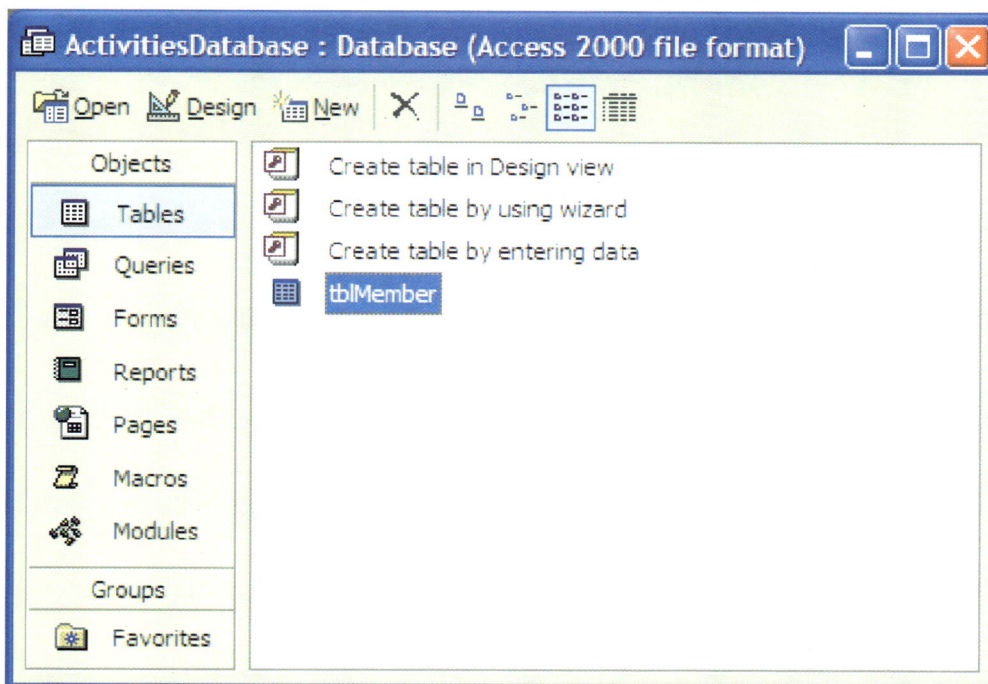

**ActivitiesDatabase : Database (Access 2000 file format)**

🗁 Open  📐 Design  ✱ New  ✕  ▫▫  ▫▫  ▦  ▦

| Objects | |
|---|---|
| ▦ Tables | 🗐 Create table in Design view |
| 🗐 Queries | 🗐 Create table by using wizard |
| 🖽 Forms | 🗐 Create table by entering data |
| 🖽 Reports | ▦ tblMember |
| 🖽 Pages | |
| 🗐 Macros | |
| 🗐 Modules | |
| Groups | |
| ▦ Favorites | |

*Figure 3.6: The Database window*

The table appears as shown below:

| MemberNo | FirstName | Surname | ContactName | ContactNo | DateOfBirth | Activity | AmountPaid | Transport? |
|---|---|---|---|---|---|---|---|---|
| 1 | John | Hainsworth | Mrs Hainsworth | 01474 678456 | 20/05/1989 | Windsurf | £0.00 | ☑ |
| 2 | Tony | Hodson | Mr Hodson | 01474 212394 | 07/09/1984 | Abseil | £15.00 | ☑ |
| 3 | Mike | Stevenson | Mr Denton | 01474 665498 | 15/11/1990 | Abseil | £20.00 | ☐ |
| 4 | Sharron | Hart | Mr Hart | 01474 374509 | 22/04/1985 | Riding | £10.00 | ☑ |
| 5 | Richard | Ellis | Mrs Muller | 01474 151884 | 12/08/1988 | Windsurf | £20.00 | ☐ |
| 6 | Lucie | Harris | Mrs Harris | 01474 908635 | 14/12/1990 | Riding | £20.00 | ☑ |
| AutoNumber | | | | | | | £0.00 | ▨ |

*Figure 3.7*

# Using the record selectors

You can move to the next or previous record using the record selectors in Datasheet View. You can also move to the first or last record, or to a new record at the end of the database. Of course with so few records in the database it is quite easy to simply click in the required row, but you must remember that real databases usually have hundreds or thousands of records, so you may need these techniques one day.

*Figure 3.8: The record selectors*

# Finding a record

Sometimes you may want to find the record for a particular member. Again, this is most useful on a much larger database.

▶ Click the mouse anywhere in the Surname column, except in Tony Hodson's record.

Suppose you want to find the record for Tony Hodson.

▶ Click the Find icon on the toolbar. ────────────── 🔍

▶ Type the name Hodson in the dialogue box, and click Find Next.

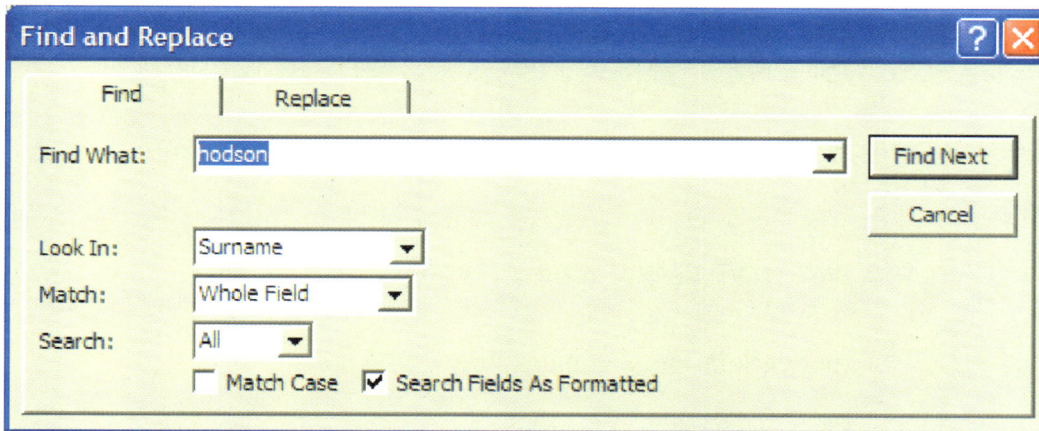

**Find and Replace**      [?][X]

| Find | Replace |
|---|---|

Find What: hodson ▼    [ Find Next ]

           [ Cancel ]

Look In: Surname ▼

Match: Whole Field ▼

Search: All ▼

☐ Match Case ☑ Search Fields As Formatted

*Figure 3.9: Finding a record*

Tony's record should now be highlighted.

▶ You can use wildcards such as * in a search. Try searching for H*.
This will find the next record starting with H each time you click
Find Next.

▶ Close the Find and Replace window by clicking its Close icon. ────── [X]

# Editing Data

You can change the contents of any field (except MemberNo
which, being an AutoNumber field, is set by Access) by clicking in
the field and editing in the normal way. Use the Backspace or
Delete key to delete unwanted text and type the corrections.

Remember you can undo changes using the Undo icon. ────────── ↰

# Adding a new record

Suppose a new member has signed up for an Activities weekend, and their details have to be added to the Activities database. Their details are shown below:

| FirstName | Surname | ContactName | ContactNo | DateOfBirth | Activity | Amount Paid | Transport? |
|-----------|---------|-------------|-----------|-------------|----------|-------------|------------|
| Eric | Fairbairn | Mrs Fairbairn | 01474 472967 | 2/9/84 | Abseil | £0 | Y |

There are two ways to add a new record:

▶ Either click in the next blank line,

▶ or press the New Record icon on either the record selector (see Figure 3.8) or the Menu bar.

▶ Enter Eric Fairbairn's details from the table above.

The first method is easy for such a small database, but if there were hundreds of members in the database you wouldn't want to scroll down to an empty row. For larger databases you would use the New Record icon.

# Deleting a record

To delete Eric Fairbairn's record:

▶ Click anywhere in Eric's record.

▶ Press the Delete icon on the toolbar. ─────────────── ▷✕

You will see a message:

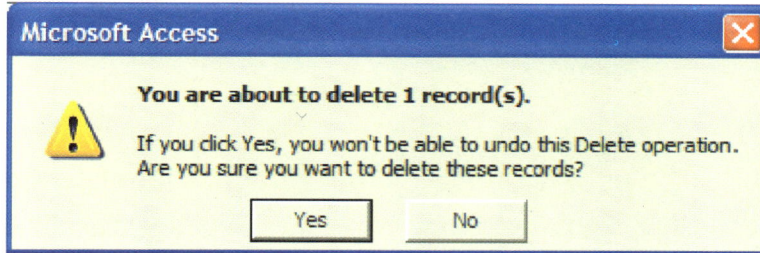

**Microsoft Access** ✕

⚠ **You are about to delete 1 record(s).**

If you click Yes, you won't be able to undo this Delete operation.
Are you sure you want to delete these records?

[ Yes ]   [ No ]

*Figure 3.10: Deleting a record*

▶ Click Yes to delete the record.

If you have added or changed any other records, restore them now
to how they are in Table 3.5. It does not matter if the MemberNo
field is different in your records.

▶ Save and close your database.

# Chapter 4
# Data Validation

It is important to make sure that you have entered the correct data into the database. If you make a mistake entering data, especially in very large databases, the error can be very difficult to trace. For example, if you entered Windsurfing instead of Windsurf as the activity for a member, then when you searched the database for all those with Windsurf as their activity, that particular member wouldn't be shown.

Although there are many errors which the database cannot detect (such as a misspelt name), there are many that it can.

You can write a set of rules which the data must abide by. For example:

- All the DateOfBirth fields must fall within a sensible range, given the ages of people in the youth club.

- Only Windsurf, Abseil, Riding or Archery can be entered in the Activity field.

- The value of AmountPaid cannot exceed a certain limit. If you know that the maximum cost of any activity won't be more than £20, you can set this as the limit.

The process of checking that the data meets various 'rules' is called validation. The rules themselves are called validation rules.

# What happens if the data doesn't match the validation rules?

Alongside each rule, you can enter some text that Access will show to the user if they enter invalid data. This is called validation text.

# Types of rule

There are various types of rule that you can enter, and they are listed in the table below.

| Operator | Meaning | Example |
|---|---|---|
| < | less than | <20 |
| <= | less than or equal to | <=20 |
| > | greater than | >0 |
| >= | greater than or equal to | >=0 |
| = | equal to | =20<br>="Windsurf" OR "Abseil" |
| <> | not equal to | <>"Windsurfing" |
| BETWEEN | test for a range of values. Must be two comparison values (a low & high value) separated by AND operator | BETWEEN 01/01/1984 AND 31/12/1991 |

*Table 4.1: Comparison operators*

# Entering the validation rules

▶ Open the file ActivitiesDatabase.

▶ In the Database window, make sure the Tables tab is selected, then click to select tblMember.

▶ Click Design to open the table in Design View. ——————— 📐 Design

We are going to enter a validation rule for the DateOfBirth field. The rule we will use is: DateOfBirth must be between 01/01/1984 and 31/12/1991.

▶ Click in the FirstName field name.

Notice that there are two rows in the field properties at the bottom of the screen named Validation Rule and Validation Text. This is where we will enter the rules.

▶ Click in the DateOfBirth field name.

▶ In the Field Properties, click in the Validation Rule row.

▶ Type Between 01/01/1984 And 31/12/1991 and press Enter.

▶ In the Validation Text row type The Date Of Birth must be between 01/01/1984 and 31/12/1991 and press Enter.

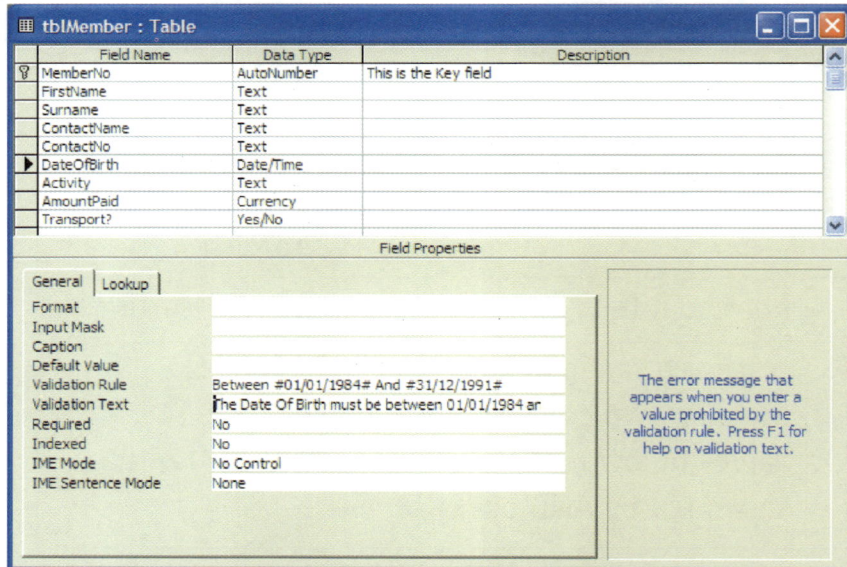

**Tip:**

You will not see these rows if the cursor is in the **MemberNo** field. You do not need validation for this field because it is an AutoNumber field.

**Tip:**

Access puts a # sign either side of each date.

| Field Name | Data Type | Description |
|---|---|---|
| MemberNo | AutoNumber | This is the Key field |
| FirstName | Text | |
| Surname | Text | |
| ContactName | Text | |
| ContactNo | Text | |
| DateOfBirth | Date/Time | |
| Activity | Text | |
| AmountPaid | Currency | |
| Transport? | Yes/No | |

Field Properties

General | Lookup

| | |
|---|---|
| Format | |
| Input Mask | |
| Caption | |
| Default Value | |
| Validation Rule | Between #01/01/1984# And #31/12/1991# |
| Validation Text | The Date Of Birth must be between 01/01/1984 ar |
| Required | No |
| Indexed | No |
| IME Mode | No Control |
| IME Sentence Mode | None |

The error message that appears when you enter a value prohibited by the validation rule. Press F1 for help on validation text.

*Figure 4.2*

▶ Return to Datasheet View by clicking the Datasheet View icon. ──────────── 🖽 ▾

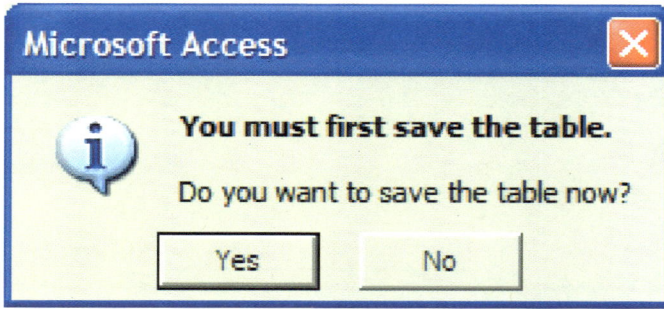

**Microsoft Access**

ⓘ You must first save the table.

Do you want to save the table now?

[ Yes ]   [ No ]

*Figure 4.3*

▶ You will be asked to save the changes you have just made. Click Yes, and Yes to the prompt about data integrity rules.

# Test the validation rule

We will test the rule by entering a new record that does not agree with the validation rule.

| FirstName | Surname | ContactName | ContactNo | DateOfBirth | Activity | Amount Paid | Transport? |
|-----------|---------|-------------|-----------|-------------|----------|-------------|------------|
| Beccy | Lock | Mrs Lock | 01474 505783 | 3/6/24 | Windsurf | £20 | Y |

▶ Click in the empty row below Lucie Harris's record and enter the FirstName as Beccy.

▶ Enter the Surname, ContactName and ContactNo for Beccy Lock as they appear in the table above.

▶ Enter the DateOfBirth as 3/6/24 and press Enter.

*Beccy Lock, world's most active Granny??*

A message will appear on the screen containing the Validation Text that you entered:

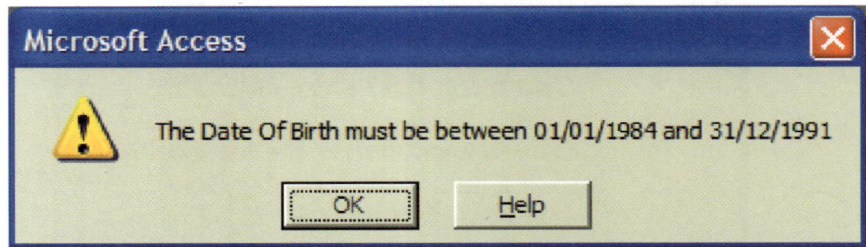

Figure 4.4

▶ Change the DateOfBirth to 3/6/84 and press Enter.

▶ Now enter the other details for Beccy Lock from the table above.

# Setting the other validation rules

Now we will set the rule for the Activity field. The rule we will use is: the activity must be one of Windsurf, Abseil, Riding or Archery.

Return to Design View by clicking the Design View icon.

▶ Click in the field name for Activity to bring up its field properties.

▶ In the Validation Rule row of the field properties type ="Windsurf" or "Abseil" or "Riding" or "Archery".

▶ In the Validation Text row type Enter Abseil, Windsurf, Riding or Archery.

Try entering a rule for the AmountPaid. The text would be something like: *AmountPaid cannot exceed £20*.

The Validation Rule would be <=20.

# More testing!

▶ Return to Datasheet View by clicking the Datasheet View icon.

▶ Click Yes to save the changes and Yes to the prompt about data integrity rules.

In the table below are more records that have to be entered.

▶ Try entering invalid values for DateOfBirth, Activity and AmountPaid. You should see your error messages appearing!

| FirstName | Surname | ContactName | ContactNo | DateOfBirth | Activity | Amount Paid | Transport? |
|-----------|---------|-------------|-----------|-------------|----------|-------------|------------|
| Omar | Iqbal | Mr Iqbal | 01474 673028 | 5/7/91 | Abseil | £10 | N |
| Gareth | Jones | Mr Jones | 01474 255836 | 26/6/85 | Windsurf | £15 | Y |
| Seb | Harris | Mr Harris | 01474 682453 | 21/6/86 | Archery | £0 | Y |

▶ When you have entered the records with the data shown, save and close your table.

▶ Close Access if this is the end of a session.

**Tip:**
Always test your validation rules by trying to enter invalid data. You can press **Esc** to cancel the record without saving it.

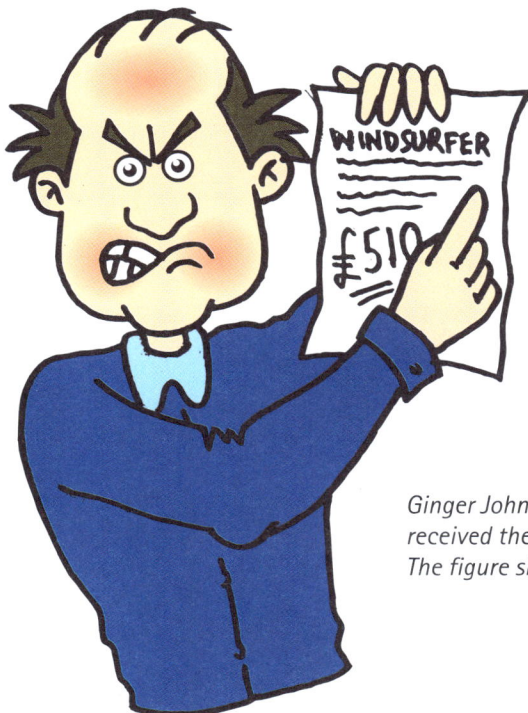

*Ginger John's dad saw red when he received the bill for John's windsurfing. The figure should have read £15.00.*

# Chapter 5

# Formatting and Printing

## Tip:

Remember you can open your table in Datasheet view by pressing **Open** in the Database window.

▶ Open the file **ActivitiesDatabase**.

▶ Double-click **tblMember** to open it.

## Sorting records

You can perform a simple sort on one field by clicking anywhere in the column you want to sort on and pressing one of the two **Sort** buttons (**Sort Ascending** and **Sort Descending**) on the toolbar.

To sort the members in the table by surname:

▶ Click in the **Surname** field and press the **Sort Ascending** icon. The records will now be sorted in ascending order of surname, as shown below.

| MemberNo | FirstName | Surname | ContactName | ContactNo | DateOfBirth | Activity | AmountPaid | Transport? |
|---|---|---|---|---|---|---|---|---|
| 5 | Richard | Ellis | Mrs Muller | 01474 151884 | 12/08/1988 | Windsurf | £20.00 | ☐ |
| 1 | John | Hainsworth | Mrs Hainsworth | 01474 678456 | 20/05/1989 | Windsurf | £0.00 | ☑ |
| 10 | Seb | Harris | Mr Harris | 01474 682453 | 21/06/1986 | Archery | £0.00 | ☑ |
| 6 | Lucie | Harris | Mrs Harris | 01474 908635 | 14/12/1990 | Riding | £20.00 | ☑ |
| 4 | Sharron | Hart | Mr Hart | 01474 374509 | 22/04/1985 | Riding | £10.00 | ☑ |
| 2 | Tony | Hodson | Mr Hodson | 01474 212394 | 07/09/1984 | Abseil | £15.00 | ☑ |
| 8 | Omar | Iqbal | Mr Iqbal | 01474 673028 | 05/07/1991 | Abseil | £10.00 | ☐ |
| 9 | Gareth | Jones | Mr Jones | 01474 255836 | 26/06/1985 | Windsurf | £15.00 | ☑ |
| 7 | Beccy | Lock | Mrs Lock | 01474 505783 | 03/06/1984 | Windsurf | £20.00 | ☑ |
| 3 | Mike | Stevenson | Mr Denton | 01474 665498 | 15/11/1990 | Abseil | £20.00 | ☐ |

Record: ◄ ◄ 1 ► ►I ►* of 10

*Figure 5.1: Records sorted by Surname*

# Formatting and printing a datasheet

You can print a datasheet just as it is, or you can format it first by hiding unwanted columns, changing the order of the columns and changing column widths. We will practise these techniques.

▶ With tblMember open in Datasheet View, click the Print Preview icon. Your data appears as shown below:

| MemberNo | FirstName | Surname | ContactName | ContactNo | DateOfBirth | Activity |
|---|---|---|---|---|---|---|
| 5 | Richard | Ellis | Mrs Muller | 01474 151884 | 12/08/1988 | Windsurf |
| 1 | John | Hainsworth | Mrs Hainsworth | 01474 678456 | 20/05/1989 | Windsurf |
| 10 | Seb | Harris | Mr Harris | 01474 682453 | 21/06/1986 | Archery |
| 6 | Lucie | Harris | Mrs Harris | 01474 908635 | 14/12/1990 | Riding |
| 4 | Sharron | Hart | Mr Hart | 01474 374509 | 22/04/1985 | Riding |
| 2 | Tony | Hodson | Mr Hodson | 01474 212394 | 07/09/1984 | Abseil |
| 8 | Omar | Iqbal | Mr Iqbal | 01474 673028 | 05/07/1991 | Abseil |
| 9 | Gareth | Jones | Mr Jones | 01474 255836 | 26/06/1985 | Windsurf |
| 7 | Beccy | Lock | Mrs Lock | 01474 505783 | 03/06/1984 | Windsurf |
| 3 | Mike | Stevenson | Mr Denton | 01474 665498 | 15/11/1990 | Abseil |

*(tblMember : Table — tblMember — 06/08/2002)*

Page: 1

Page selector

*Figure 5.2: Print preview of the datasheet*

**Tip:**
If it's too small to read, click on it to enlarge it

You will notice that the whole datasheet will not fit on one page in Portrait view. You can use the page selector at the bottom of the screen to view the second page.

The Print Preview toolbar appears at the top of the screen. Using tools on this toolbar you can see both pages of this report. You can Zoom in on a page by clicking anywhere on it, or by clicking the Zoom icon.

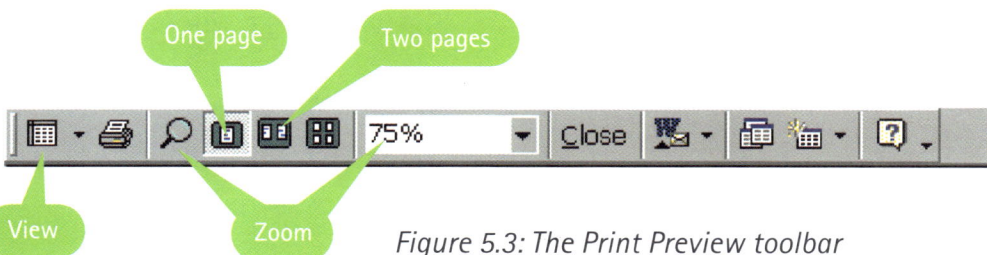

One page    Two pages

View    Zoom    75%    Close

*Figure 5.3: The Print Preview toolbar*

▶ Click the View icon to return to Datasheet View.

# Changing the Page layout

You can change the page layout to Landscape view.

▶ Select File, Page Setup... from the menu.

▶ Click the Page tab in the Page Setup dialogue box. Click Landscape.

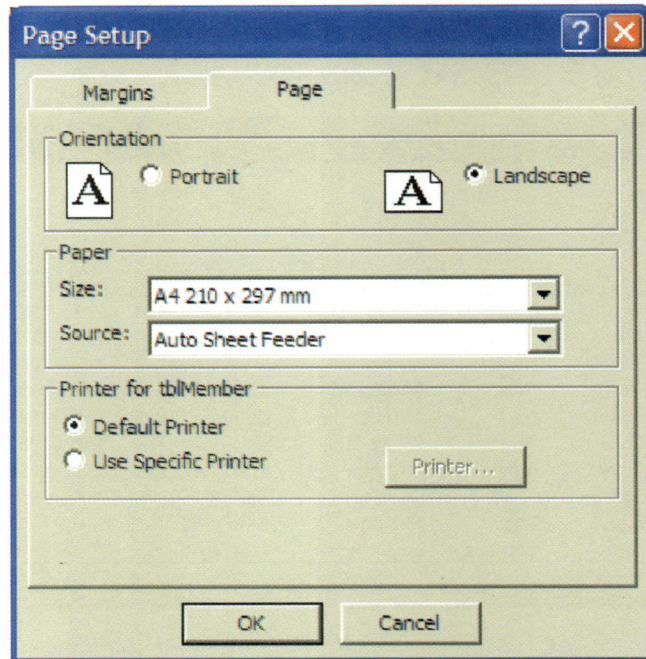

*Figure 5.4: Page setup dialogue box*

▶ Try another Print Preview. This time it should fit on a single page.

# Hiding and Unhiding columns

Sometimes you may not want to print all the columns in the datasheet. You can hide the columns that you don't want.

▶ Make sure you have tblMember open in Datasheet View.

▶ Drag across the column headers AmountPaid and Transport?.

▶ From the menu select Format, Hide Columns. The columns will now be hidden.

**Tip:**
To unhide the columns you select **Format, Unhide Columns**.

# Formatting columns

Suppose you want to put the DateOfBirth column right at the end.

▶ Click the DateOfBirth column header to select the column.

▶ Click again and hold down the mouse button, then drag the header to the end of the table.

▶ Adjust the column widths by double-clicking in the column header on the border between each column.

Your table should now appear as shown below.

> Drag the column header to move the column

| MemberNo | FirstName | Surname | ContactName | ContactNo | Activity | DateOfBirth |
|---|---|---|---|---|---|---|
| 5 | Richard | Ellis | Mrs Muller | 01474 151884 | Windsurf | 12/08/1988 |
| 1 | John | Hainsworth | Mrs Hainsworth | 01474 678456 | Windsurf | 20/05/1989 |
| 10 | Seb | Harris | Mr Harris | 01474 682453 | Archery | 21/06/1986 |
| 6 | Lucie | Harris | Mrs Harris | 01474 908635 | Riding | 14/12/1990 |
| 4 | Sharron | Hart | Mr Hart | 01474 374509 | Riding | 22/04/1985 |
| 2 | Tony | Hodson | Mr Hodson | 01474 212394 | Abseil | 07/09/1984 |
| 8 | Omar | Iqbal | Mr Iqbal | 01474 673028 | Abseil | 05/07/1991 |
| 9 | Gareth | Jones | Mr Jones | 01474 255836 | Windsurf | 26/06/1985 |
| 7 | Beccy | Lock | Mrs Lock | 01474 505783 | Windsurf | 03/06/1984 |
| 3 | Mike | Stevenson | Mr Denton | 01474 665498 | Abseil | 15/11/1990 |

Record: 1 of 10

*Figure 5.5*

▶ Click the Print Preview icon again to see what the page will look like when printed out.

▶ Click the Close icon and click Yes when asked if you want to save changes to the table layout.

# Chapter 6

# Making Queries

One of the most useful things you can do with a database is to find all the records that satisfy a certain condition, such as "All the members who are going windsurfing".

This is called querying the database.

▶ Load Access and open ActivitiesDatabase.

## Creating a new query

Queries
▶ In the Database window, click Queries in the list of objects on the left of the screen.

New
▶ Select New at the top of the window.

▶ In the next window, select Design View. Click OK.

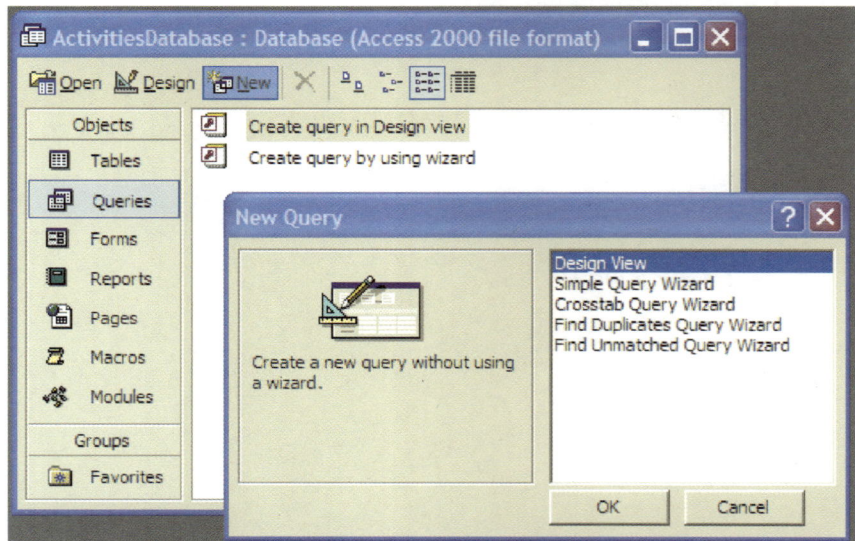

*Figure 6.1: Designing a new query*

▶ In the Show Table dialogue box, click Add and then click Close.

# Selecting fields to appear in the query

A query grid appears. You need to place selected fields onto the grid from the tblMember table. These will be fields for which you want to specify conditions, called criteria.

▶ In the tblMember pane in the upper half of the window, double-click in turn the fields FirstName, Surname, DateOfBirth and Activity. As you double-click the fields, they will be placed in the query grid.

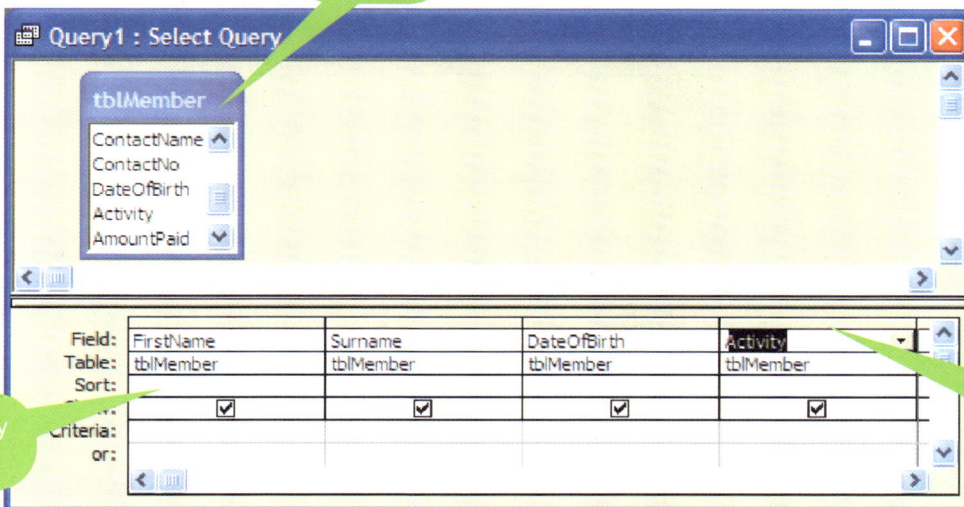

Tip:
To place a field in the query grid you can either double-click the field in the tblMember pane, or drag it onto the query grid.

*Figure 6.2: Specifying fields and criteria*

Suppose you now want to delete the DateOfBirth field from the query.

▶ Click in the column header of the DateOfBirth field to select the column and press the Delete key.

To add the Transport? field to your query:

▶ Click and drag Transport? from the tblMember pane and put it on top of the next blank field on the right. It will be inserted in that field.

# Setting simple criteria

Now suppose you want to find all the members who have chosen windsurfing as their preferred activity.

▶ In the Criteria row of the Activity column, enter "Windsurf".

▶ Now run your query to see the results. Click the Run icon on the toolbar.

The results appear as shown below.

| FirstName | Surname | Activity | Transport? |
|---|---|---|---|
| John | Hainsworth | Windsurf | ☑ |
| Richard | Ellis | Windsurf | ☐ |
| Beccy | Lock | Windsurf | ☑ |
| Gareth | Jones | Windsurf | ☑ |

Record: 1 of 4

*Figure 6.3: The query results table*

# Saving a query

You can save a query so that it can be run whenever you like. For example, after you have added more records to the database, you may want to search it again for windsurfing members.

Saving the query saves the question not the answer table.

▶ Click the Save icon to save the query.

▶ Save it as qryWindsurf.

# Multiple Criteria

Suppose you wanted to find all the members signed up for either windsurfing or abseiling. You will notice that the row under Criteria is headed or.

▶ Return to Design View to change the query. ──────────

▶ In the row headed or, under the criteria "Windsurf", type "Abseil".

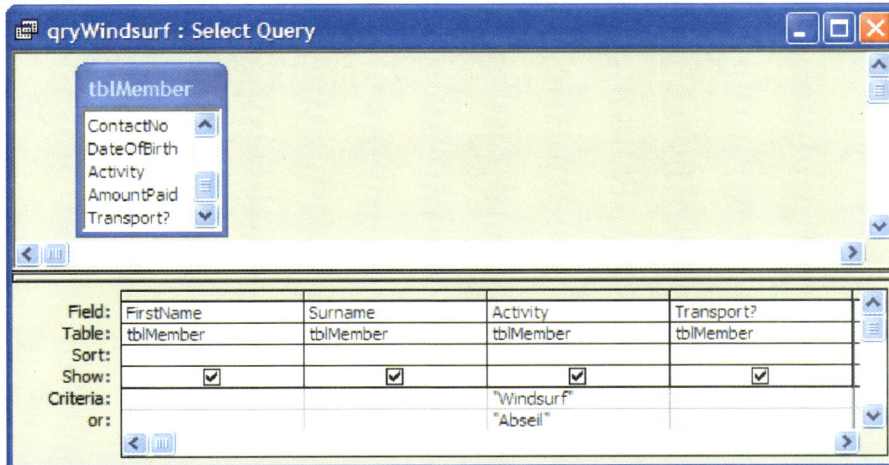

| Field: | FirstName | Surname | Activity | Transport? |
|---|---|---|---|---|
| Table: | tblMember | tblMember | tblMember | tblMember |
| Sort: | | | | |
| Show: | ☑ | ☑ | ☑ | ☑ |
| Criteria: | | | "Windsurf" | |
| or: | | | "Abseil" | |

*Figure 6.4: Setting multiple criteria*

▶ Run the query again. ──────────

The query results table should now look like this:

| | FirstName | Surname | Activity | Transport? |
|---|---|---|---|---|
| ▶ | John | Hainsworth | Windsurf | ☑ |
| | Tony | Hodson | Abseil | ☑ |
| | Mike | Stevenson | Abseil | ☐ |
| | Richard | Ellis | Windsurf | ☐ |
| | Beccy | Lock | Windsurf | ☑ |
| | Omar | Iqbal | Abseil | ☐ |
| | Gareth | Jones | Windsurf | ☑ |
| * | | | | |

Record: ◀◀ ◀ 1 ▶ ▶◀ ▶* of 7

*Figure 6.5: The query results table*

▶ Select File, Save As from the menu bar.

▶ Save your query as qryWindsurf&Abseil.

▶ Close your query.

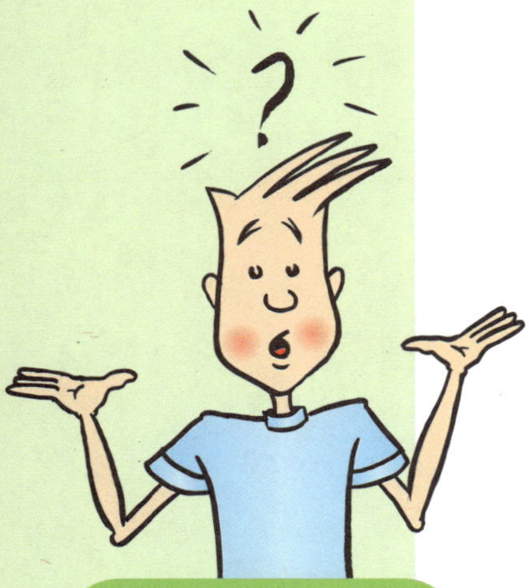

# Using comparison operators

Sometimes you need to find all records with a field less than or greater than a particular value. You can use any of the operators that you used in Chapter 4 for validating data. Look back at them to remind yourself what they were!

We will search for all members signed up for windsurfing and abseiling whose dates of births are between 1/1/1985 and 31/12/1991.

▶ Create a new query that looks like the one below.

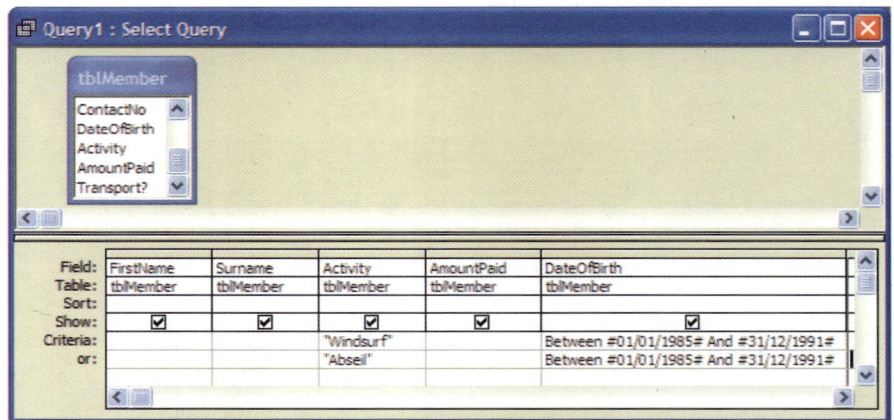

| Field: | FirstName | Surname | Activity | AmountPaid | DateOfBirth |
|---|---|---|---|---|---|
| Table: | tblMember | tblMember | tblMember | tblMember | tblMember |
| Sort: | | | | | |
| Show: | ☑ | ☑ | ☑ | ☑ | ☑ |
| Criteria: | | | "Windsurf" | | Between #01/01/1985# And #31/12/1991# |
| or: | | | "Abseil" | | Between #01/01/1985# And #31/12/1991# |

*Figure 6.6*

▶ Run the query.

The results should look like this:

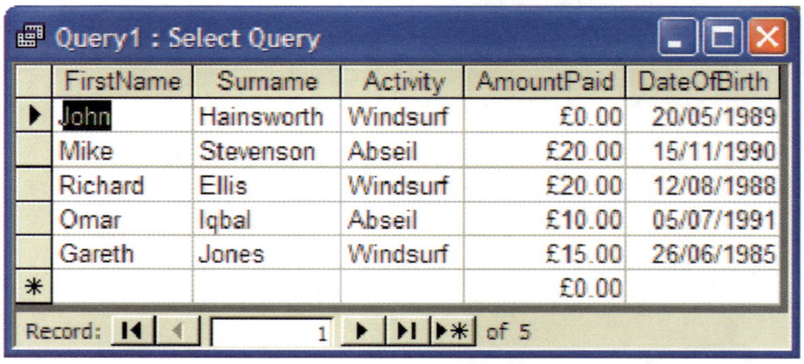

| FirstName | Surname | Activity | AmountPaid | DateOfBirth |
|---|---|---|---|---|
| John | Hainsworth | Windsurf | £0.00 | 20/05/1989 |
| Mike | Stevenson | Abseil | £20.00 | 15/11/1990 |
| Richard | Ellis | Windsurf | £20.00 | 12/08/1988 |
| Omar | Iqbal | Abseil | £10.00 | 05/07/1991 |
| Gareth | Jones | Windsurf | £15.00 | 26/06/1985 |

Record: 1 of 5

*Figure 6.7*

▶ Save the query as qryActivity&Date, without closing it.

▶ Return to Design View.

# Sorting records

Suppose you want to sort the query results by Activity.

▶ Click in the Sort row in the Activity column and select Ascending.

▶ Run the query to see the result. You will see that the records are now sorted in Activity order.

If you now wanted the members in each Activity sorted in Surname order:

▶ Click in the Sort row in the Surname column and select Ascending.

▶ Run the query.

| | FirstName | Surname | Activity | AmountPaid | DateOfBirth |
|---|---|---|---|---|---|
| ▶ | Richard | Ellis | Windsurf | £20.00 | 12/08/1988 |
| | John | Hainsworth | Windsurf | £0.00 | 20/05/1989 |
| | Omar | Iqbal | Abseil | £10.00 | 05/07/1991 |
| | Gareth | Jones | Windsurf | £15.00 | 26/06/1985 |
| | Mike | Stevenson | Abseil | £20.00 | 15/11/1990 |
| * | | | | £0.00 | |

Record: 1 of 5

*Figure 6.8: The table sorted by Surname*

This is not quite what we want. Access is automatically sorting by Surname before Activity. By default, Access uses the column order to decide the sort sequence.

To sort by Activity then Surname:

▶ Return to Design View.

▶ Place the cursor over the Activity column header and the cursor should change to a small down arrow. Now click to select the column.

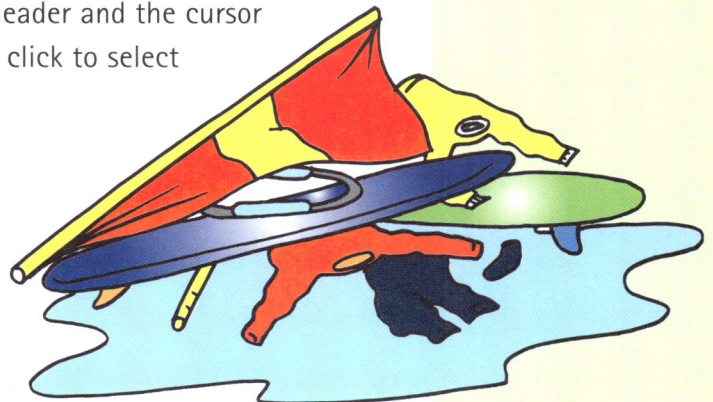

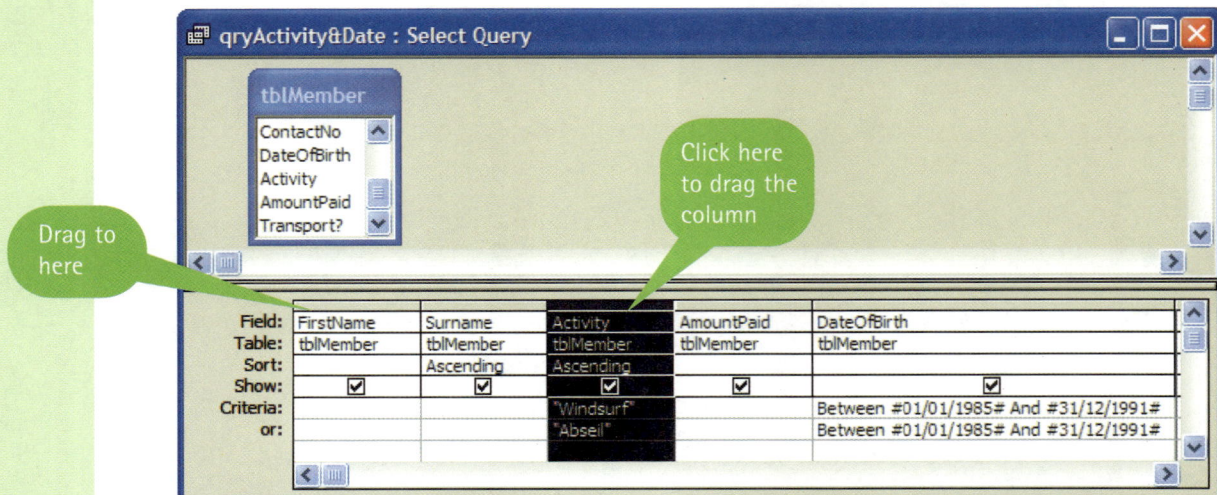

*Figure 6.9: Changing the column order*

▶ Click and drag the grey bar at the top of the **Activity** column to the left of the **FirstName** column.

▶ Run the query, and you will see that the records are now sorted in **Activity** then **Surname** order.

*Figure 6.10: Query results sorted by Activity then Surname*

# Hiding fields

Suppose you decide you do not need the AmountPaid field in this particular report.

- Return to Design View.
- Click on the Show box in the AmountPaid column to deselect it.
- Run the query again. It should appear as shown below:

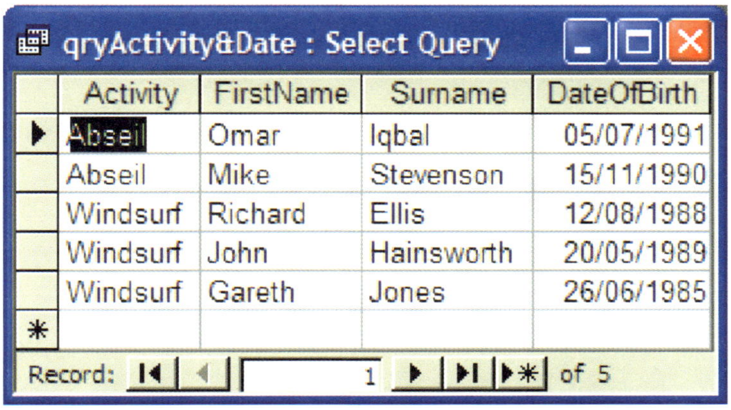

qryActivity&Date : Select Query

| Activity | FirstName | Surname | DateOfBirth |
|---|---|---|---|
| Abseil | Omar | Iqbal | 05/07/1991 |
| Abseil | Mike | Stevenson | 15/11/1990 |
| Windsurf | Richard | Ellis | 12/08/1988 |
| Windsurf | John | Hainsworth | 20/05/1989 |
| Windsurf | Gareth | Jones | 26/06/1985 |

Record: 1 of 5

*Figure 6.11: Query results with AmountPaid column hidden*

- Select File, Save from the menu to save the modified query.

# Printing your query

- You can do a Print Preview by pressing the Print Preview icon. The page layout can be altered as you did with the table in Formatting and Printing (Chapter 5).

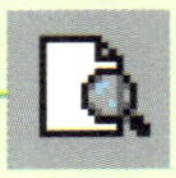

- Save and close the query.
- Close the database by selecting File, Close from the menu bar.

# Chapter **7**
# Presenting Data

Suppose you want to present the data in a table or query in a neater way, for example with a proper title and date. For this you would use a Report. Reports allow you to present data in a wide variety of ways. They can be based on queries or on tables.

▶ Load Access and select Open an existing file, then find the file ActivitiesDatabase in the box below. It should be in a folder named YouthClub.

▶ Click OK.

## Making a report

The youth club leader needs a register of all members going on the windsurfing weekend. Remember that you created qryWindsurf in the last chapter, which contained only those members whose activity was windsurfing. Our report will be based on this query.

Reports ────▶ In the Database window, select the Reports tab.

▶ Double-click Create report by using wizard. (You could also select New, Report wizard.)

▶ In the Tables/Queries drop-down list select qryWindsurf.

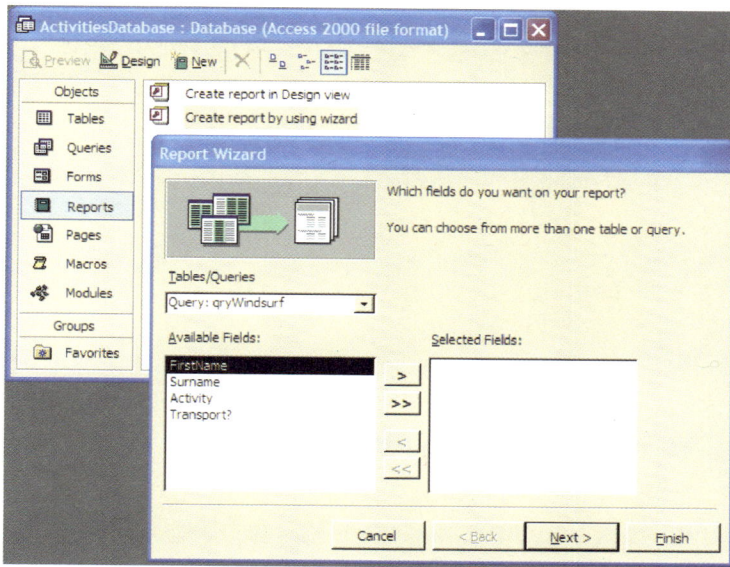

*Figure 7.1*

In the box below will be a list of all the (unhidden) fields in the query. Highlight FirstName and click > to make it appear in the report.

Repeat this for Surname and Transport?.

We will leave Activity out of the report because we know that all the members will be doing windsurfing.

Click Next.

The next dialogue box will ask about grouping levels. The youth club leader would find it useful to have the members grouped by who needs transport.

Click Transport? so that it is highlighted, then click >.

Click Next.

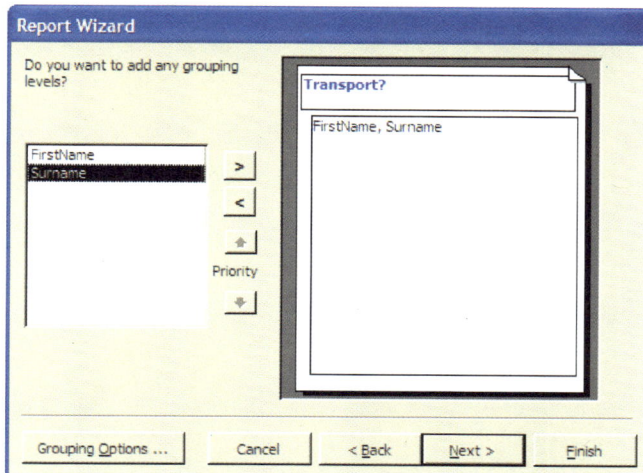

*Figure 7.2*

Now you are asked for a sort order. We want the members in Surname, then FirstName order.

▶ In the first drop-down list select Surname.

▶ In the second drop-down list select FirstName.

The next two dialogue boxes are about the format and style of the report. We will leave these as they are for now.

▶ Click Next three more times, until Access asks What title do you want for your report?

▶ Enter rptWindsurf then click Finish.

The report, saved as rptWindsurf, should appear as shown below:

**Tip:**

By default, Access saves the report under the name that you give for the title. The common naming convention is to save reports with a name beginning **rpt.**

| rptWindsurf | | |
|---|---|---|

| Transport? | Surname | FirstName |
|---|---|---|
| Yes | | |
| | Hainsworth | John |
| | Jones | Gareth |
| | Lock | Beccy |
| No | | |
| | Ellis | Richard |

Page: 1

*Figure 7.3*

46

# Editing the report format

To format the report you use Design View.

Notice that in the open report the entry Yes in the Transport? field appears too far to the right of the Transport? title.

▶ Click the Design View icon. ——————————————————————

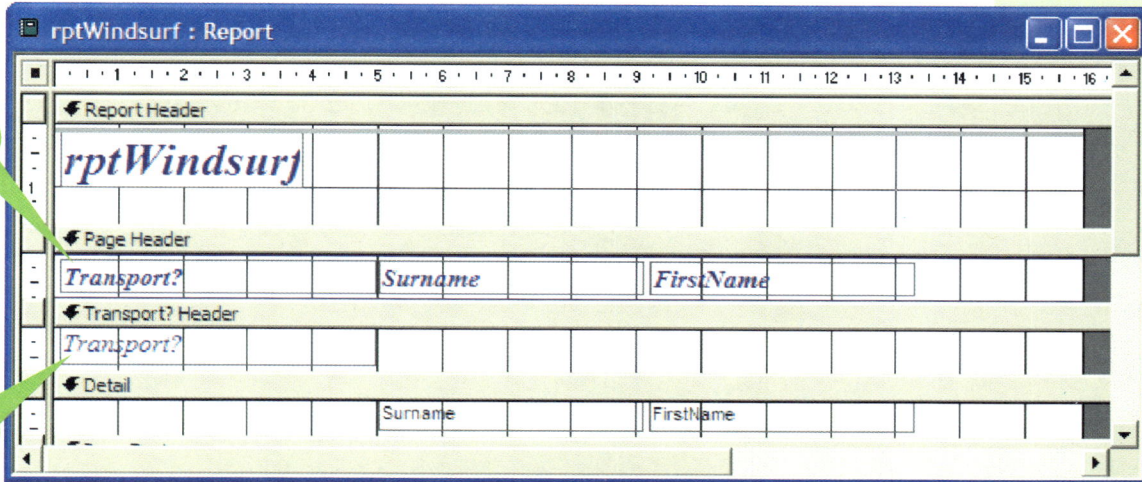

Figure 7.4

▶ Click in the Transport? field (note, you want the field, not the label. The field is the one that isn't in bold).

▶ In the toolbar at the top of the screen, click the Align Left icon. ——

▶ Return to Print Preview by clicking the Print Preview icon and ——— check that Yes appears in the right place.

# Changing the titles

At the moment the title of the report is rptWindsurf. To change the title to Windsurfing Activity Weekend:

▶ Return to Design View.

▶ Click in the box that says rptWindsurf. Click again and the text cursor should appear in the box.

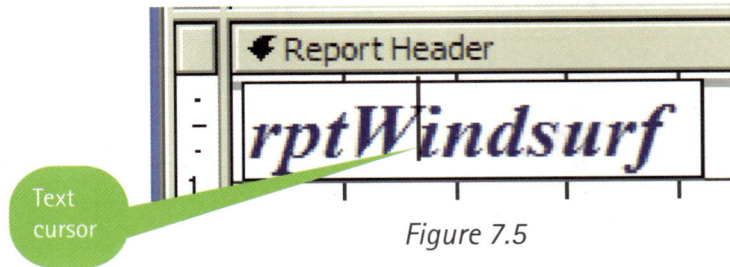

*Figure 7.5*

You can now edit the text.

▶ Change the title from rptWindsurf to Windsurfing Activity Weekend.

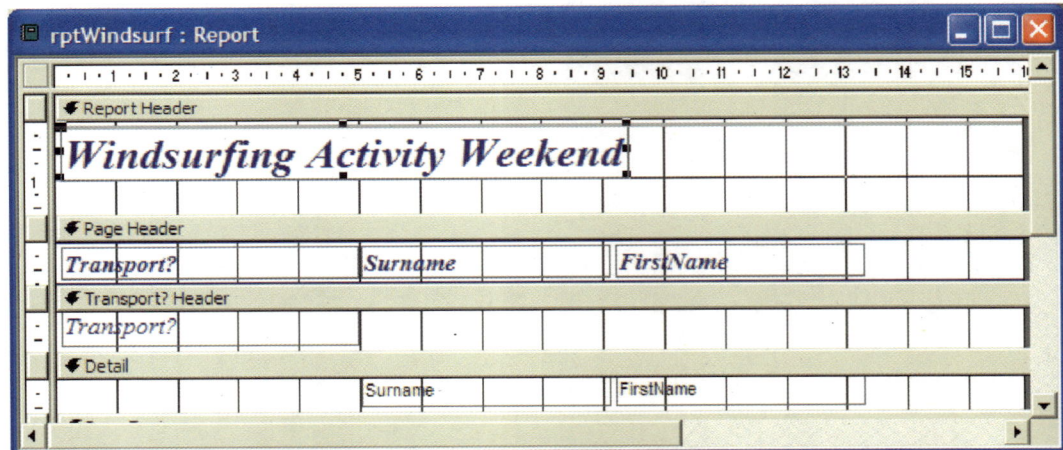

*Figure 7.6*

▶ Click the Print Preview icon and check that the report looks the way you want.

# Adding fields to the report

It would be useful, when the list of members on the Windsurfing weekend gets longer, to have a Total field which counts the number of members on the weekend.

▶ Make sure the report is in Design View.

We want to put the total in the Report Footer – don't worry that there's no white page there yet.

▶ Click the Text Box icon in the Toolbox and a little ab should appear by the cursor.

**ab|**

**Tip:**
The toolbox may appear as a toolbar. If you drag it down, it changes shape.

▶ Click below the report footer and drag to make a rectangular field.

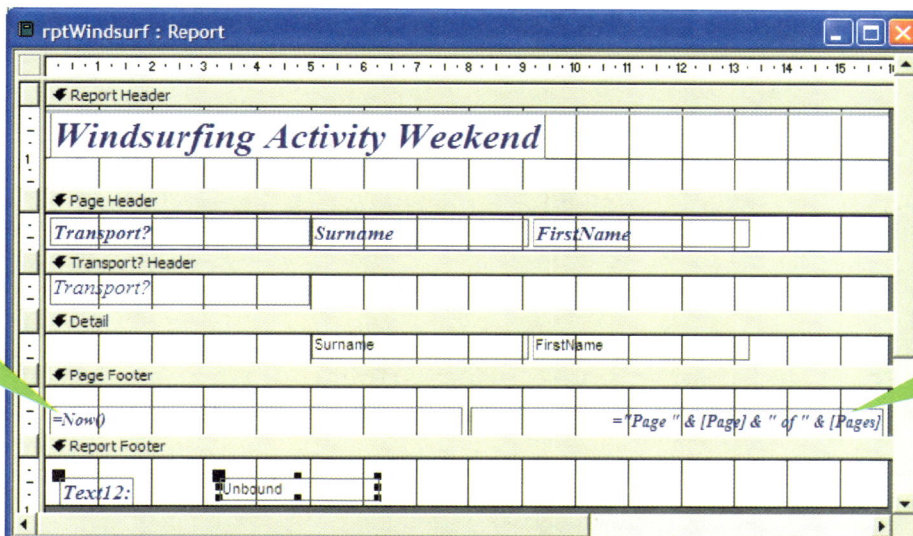

Gives today's date

Gives page number and total number of pages in the report

*Figure 7.7*

You will see that a Properties window for the text box appears. If this window does not automatically appear:

▶ Right-click the text box (the box containing Unbound).

▶ Select **Properties** from the pop-up menu.

In the **Properties** box, the text box will have a **Name** property something like **Text12** (the number may be different in your database).

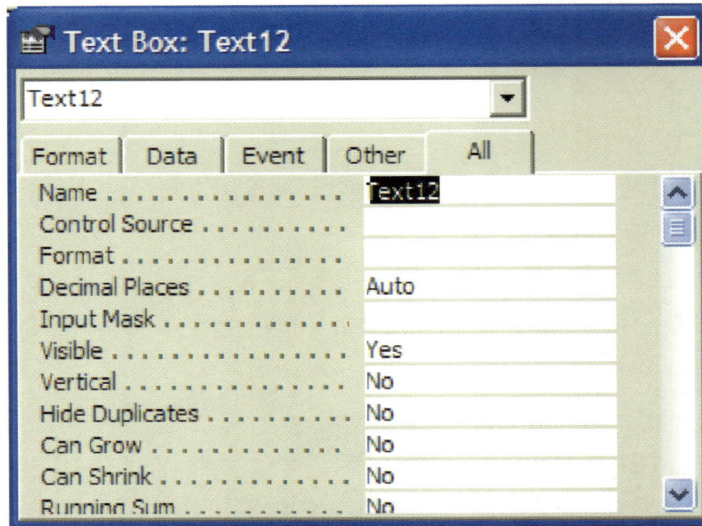

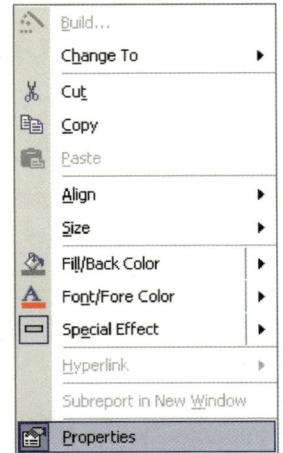

| Build... | |
| --- | --- |
| Change To | ▶ |
| ✂ Cut | |
| ▣ Copy | |
| ▣ Paste | |
| Align | ▶ |
| Size | ▶ |
| Fill/Back Color | ▶ |
| Font/Fore Color | ▶ |
| Special Effect | ▶ |
| Hyperlink | ▶ |
| Subreport in New Window | |
| Properties | |

**Text Box: Text12** ✕

Text12 ▾

| Format | Data | Event | Other | All |

Name . . . . . . . . . . . . . . . . . Text12
Control Source . . . . . . . . . .
Format . . . . . . . . . . . . . . .
Decimal Places . . . . . . . . . . Auto
Input Mask . . . . . . . . . . . . .
Visible . . . . . . . . . . . . . . . . Yes
Vertical . . . . . . . . . . . . . . . No
Hide Duplicates . . . . . . . . . . No
Can Grow . . . . . . . . . . . . . No
Can Shrink . . . . . . . . . . . . . No
Running Sum . . . . . . . . . . . No

*Figure 7.8*

▶ Change the name of the text box to **Total**.

▶ In the **Control Source** property enter **=Count(\*)**. This counts the number of records in the report, which equals the number of people on the Activities Weekend.

▶ Click on the **Text12** label on the form, then click again to edit the text. Change it to say **Total**.

▶ Return to **Print Preview** to check the results.

If you would like to tidy up the appearance of the report, you can return to **Design View** and change fonts, add lines and do various other things using the Formatting toolbar at the top of the screen.

# Printing your report

▶ In **Print Preview** view, either click the **Print** icon or go to **File**, **Print**.

▶ Save and close your report.

# Creating a bar chart

It is possible to create a report that represents selected information as a graph. Although this sounds complicated, it is easy to create a simple graph using the Chart Wizard.

We will create a chart to show the number of members taking each activity.

▶ In the Database window, make sure the Reports tab is selected and click New. ————————

New

▶ In the New Report dialogue box, select Chart Wizard.

▶ In the drop-down list in the bottom of the window select tblMember, and press OK.

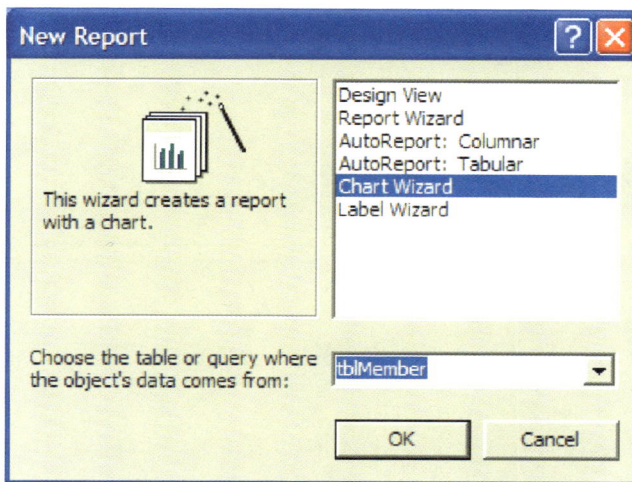

Figure 7.9

▶ In the Chart Wizard dialogue box, click to select Activity from the list of Available Fields on the left.

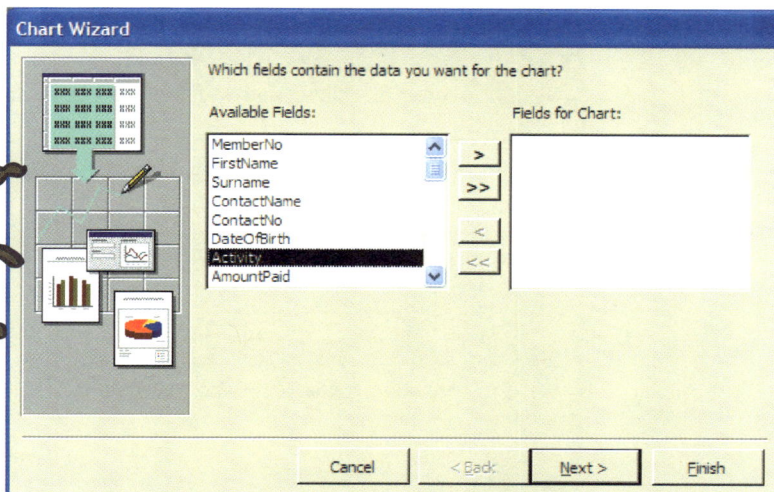

Figure 7.10

▶ Click > so that the field appears under **Fields for Chart** on the right. Click **Next**.

You are now given a choice of several different types of graph. For this example, a bar chart is a good way of representing the information.

▶ In Access, bar charts are called Column Charts. **Column Chart** should already be selected in the top left of the window, so just click **Next**.

▶ In the next window, the graph is automatically set out how we would like, so just click **Next**.

*Figure 7.11*

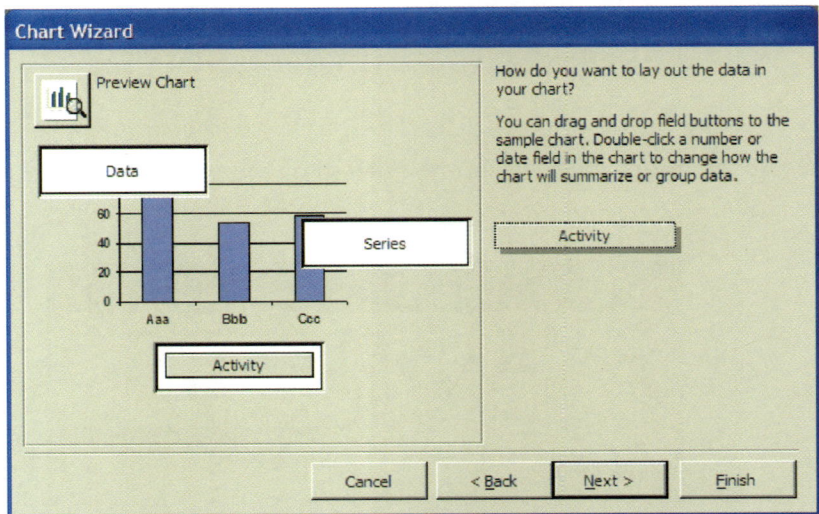

▶ Type **Activities Chart** as the title for your report.

▶ Just below where you typed the chart title, click on the option **No, don't display a legend**.

▶ Click **Finish**.

Your chart should now appear as a Print Preview.

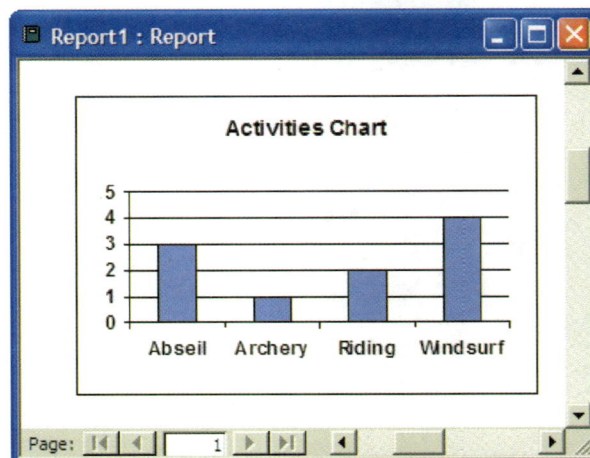

*Figure 7.12*

Now save your report.

▶ Go to File, Save from the top menu bar.

▶ Save your report as rptActivitiesChart.

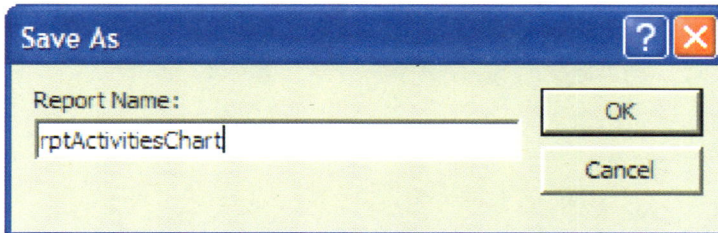

*Figure 7.13*

You can print your chart just like you printed your first report. Either select File, Print from the top menu bar, or click the Print icon.

# Creating a pie chart

Now let's try a pie chart. A pie chart shows the same information as a bar chart but in a different form. It is very easy to see, for example, whether about half of all the children are doing windsurfing.

▶ As before, go to the Database window and make sure the Reports tab is selected. Click New.

▶ Select Chart Wizard, and in the drop-down list below, select tblMember. Click OK.

▶ In the next window, select Activity from the left hand list, and click > to add it to Fields for Chart. Click Next.

This time we will select Pie Chart. Pie chart is the circle in the bottom left of the window. If you are unsure, just look at the chart name and explanation on the right of all the pictures.

▶ Click the Pie Chart button then click Next.

Now we get a chance to preview the chart (we could also have done this when we created the bar chart).

▶ In the top left, click the Preview Chart button.

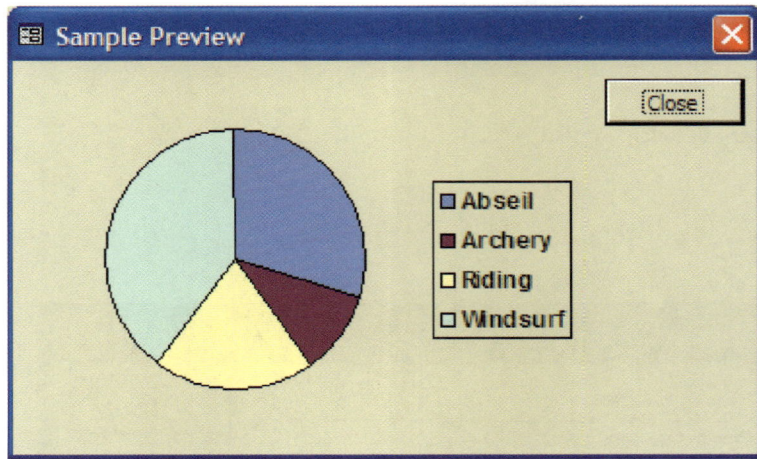

*Figure 7.14*

The Sample Preview window will appear.

▶ Click Close to return to the Chart Wizard.

▶ Click Next. Type Activities Pie Chart for the chart title.

▶ This time we do want a legend, so leave that option selected. Click Finish.

The chart should appear as shown below.

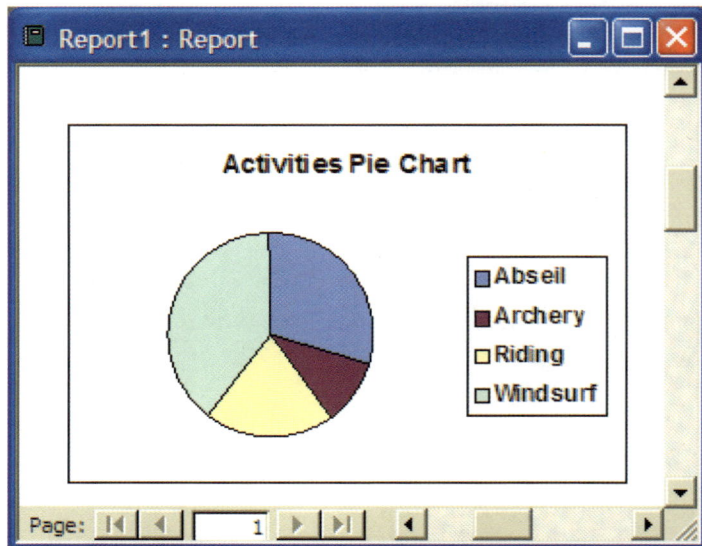

*Figure 7.15*

▶ Save your report by selecting File, Save from the menu.

▶ Save your report as rptActivitiesPieChart.

▶ Close your report by pressing the close icon (x) in the top right of the window.

If you make a mistake in your chart it is possible to edit it in Design View, but it's probably easier just to start the Chart Wizard again!

# Chapter **8**
# Forms for Data Entry

Forms are used to create a 'user interface'. They allow database users to type data into a database using a specially designed form, rather than straight into a table.

As well as providing an easy way of entering data, you can also tailor forms to accept only certain information, or only information in the correct format. This is another method of data validation.

# Creating a form

We will create a form to enter all the members and their details. This form will be used for entering data into the tblMember table.

▶ In the Database window click the Forms tab.

▶ Double-click Create form by using wizard, or click New, then Form Wizard.

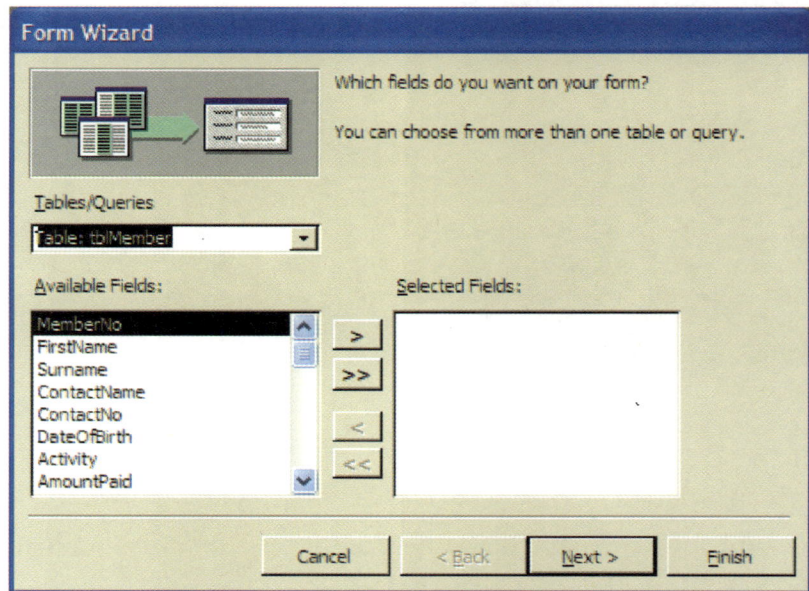

*Figure 8.1*

 In the Tables/Queries drop-down list select Table: tblMember.

 The box below contains all the fields in tblMember. We want all the fields to appear on the form, so press >> to move all the fields to the Selected Fields box on the right.

 Click Next. Leave the layout as Columnar, and click Next again.

 You are now asked which style you would like. Have a look at the previewed styles, then select Standard and click Next.

 Save the form as frmMember, and click Finish.

Your form should appear like the one below:

**Note:**

You may have a different record showing.

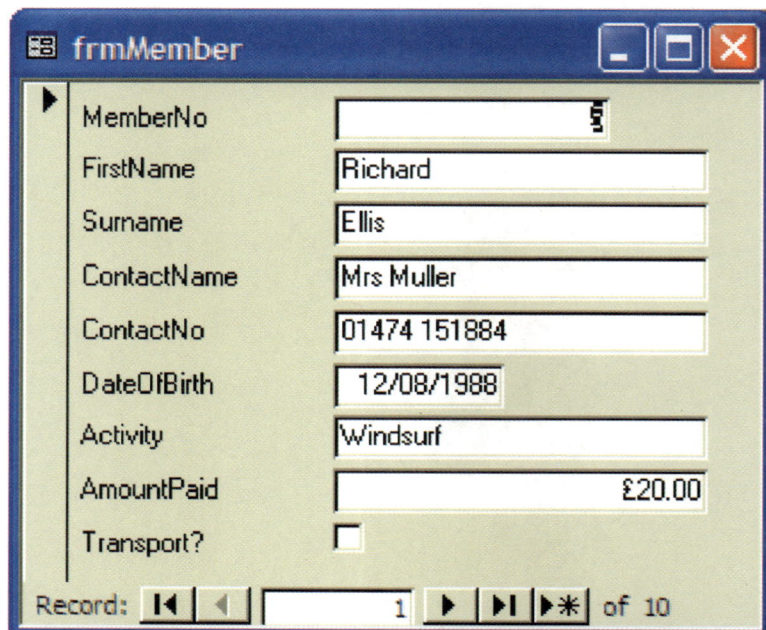

*Figure 8.2*

56

The form contains all the records that are already entered in tblMember. To switch between records use the record selectors at the bottom of the form.

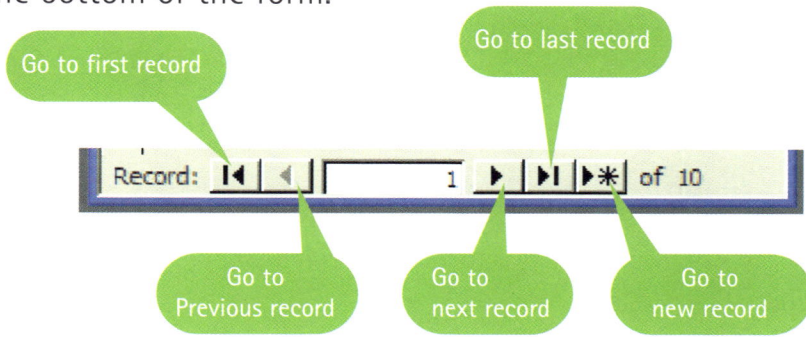

*Figure 8.3*

# Entering a record using the form

▶ Using the record selectors, click the New Record icon.

A blank form will be displayed.

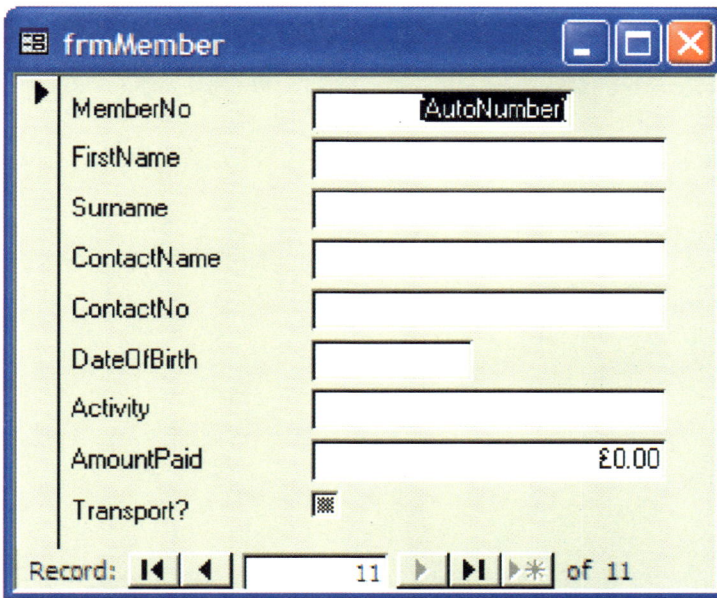

*Figure 8.4*

▶ Enter the following member:

| FirstName | Surname | ContactName | ContactNo | DateOfBirth | Activity | Amount Paid | Transport? |
|-----------|---------|-------------|-----------|-------------|----------|-------------|------------|
| Paul | Naish | Mrs Naish | 01474 358695 | 16/8/88 | Archery | £5 | Y |

# Making data entry quicker

Since there are only four choices of activity, it would be convenient to select the activity from a drop-down list.

There are two options here:

A List box shows a box on screen displaying some or all the options (no drop-down list);

A Combo box shows just one value at a time. To view all the options you click in the box to view the drop-down list.

We will use a Combo box.

# Combo boxes

Go to Design View by clicking the Design View icon.

Make the form about twice as wide by dragging out the right border.

Click the Combo Box icon in the Toolbox.

Click about a field's width to the right of the Activity field, and drag out a rectangle.

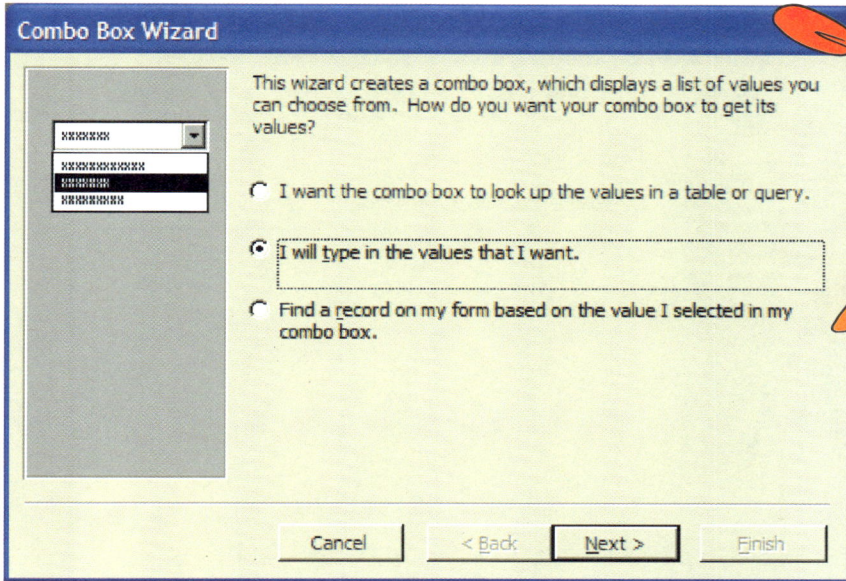

*Figure 8.5*

▶ Select the middle option I will type in the values that I want. Click Next.

▶ Leave the number of columns as 1. In the box below type in the activities: Abseil, Windsurf, Riding, Archery.

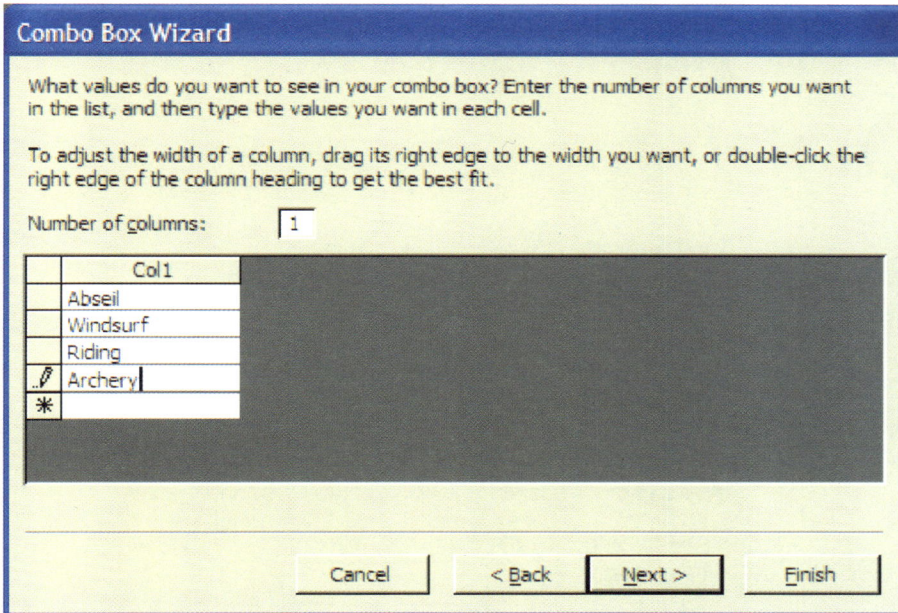

*Figure 8.6*

▶ Click Next. In the next box, select Store that value in this field and choose Activity as the field from the drop-down list. Click Next.

**Tip:**
Press **Tab** or the down arrow to get to the next line. If you press **Enter**, Access will move onto the next screen. If this happens, just press the **Back** button.

*Figure 8.7*

▶ Save the combo box as Activity and click Finish.

You now need to delete the old Activity field and put the combo box in its place:

▶ Click on the old Activity field and press the Delete key. Both the field and the label will disappear.

▶ Move the combo box and its label into place by clicking them once, then clicking and dragging when the cursor turns into a small hand.

▶ Click the Form View icon to return to Form View.

▶ You can now see there is a drop-down list containing all four activities. Click its Down arrow to show them.

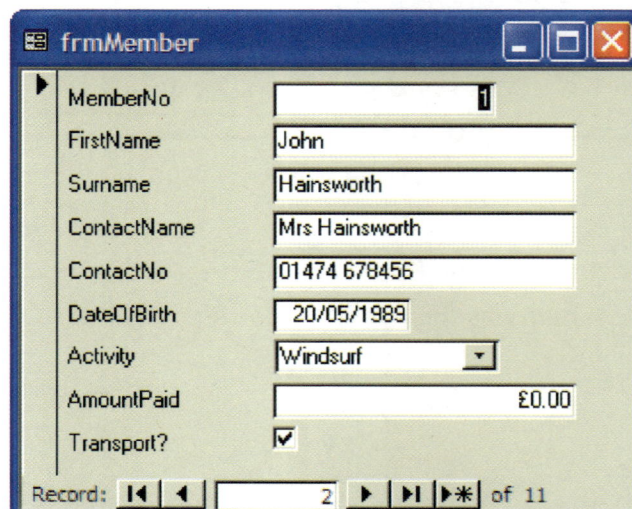

*Figure 8.8*

**Tip:**
To move the label without the box, click the label, then hover the mouse over the top left hand corner until the cursor changes to a pointing finger. Now click and drag.

If you click and drag when the cursor is not a hand you will change the shape of the box.

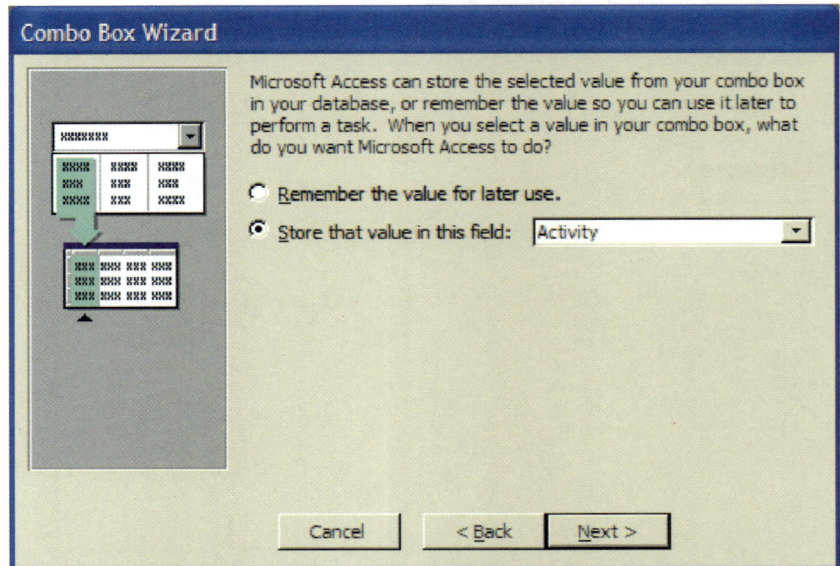

# Setting a default value

You can specify values for fields before the user has typed anything. For example, since most members require transport, it would make sense to make the default value Yes.

▶ Go to Design View.

▶ If the Properties dialogue box is not already open, open it by clicking the Properties icon in the Form Design toolbar. ─────────────

▶ Click on the Transport? field on the form and the Properties box should display the properties of this field. (Make sure you have selected the field, not the label).

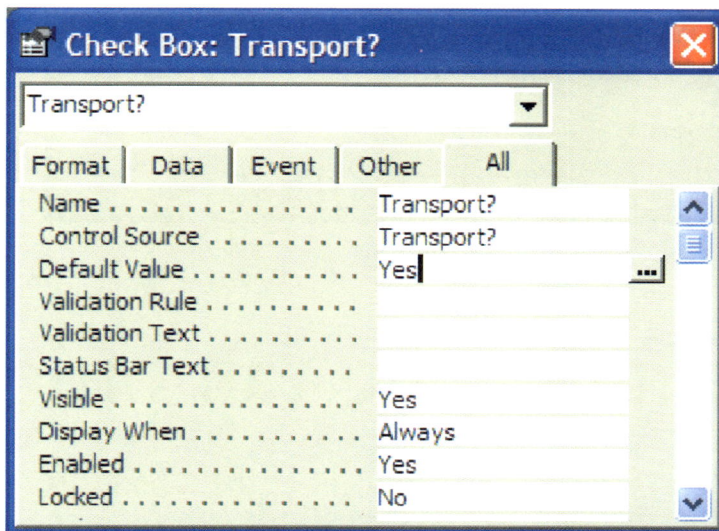

*Figure 8.9*

**Tip:**
You could also use the record selector at the bottom of the form to add a new record.

▶ In the Default Value row in the Properties box, type Yes.

▶ Go to Form View. ──────────────

▶ Click the New Record icon on the Form Design toolbar at the top of ───────── the screen.

You are now going to enter a new record using the features you have just added.

▶ Enter the following member into the form:

| FirstName | Surname | ContactName | ContactNo | DateOfBirth | Activity | Amount Paid | Transport? |
|-----------|---------|-------------|-----------|-------------|----------|-------------|------------|
| Rachel | Sandbrook | Mrs Sandbrook | 01474 498365 | 28/5/86 | Windsurf | £15 | Y |

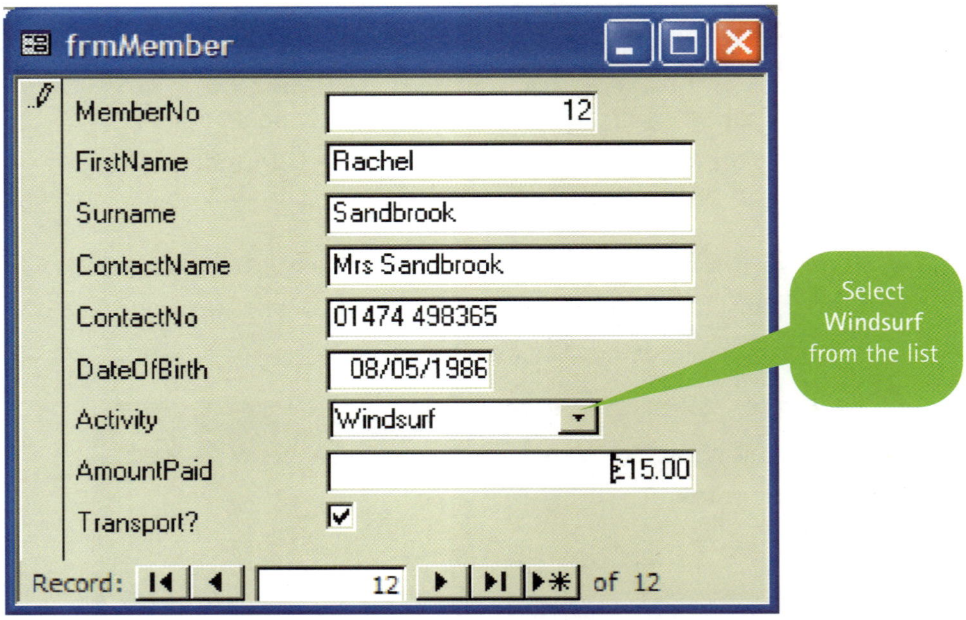

*Figure 8.10*

# Changing the tab order

Did you notice that the cursor went to the AmountPaid field before the Activity field? This is because we added the Activity field after the other fields. It would be more convenient if the cursor automatically visited the fields in the order they appear on the form.

▶ Return to Design View by clicking the Design View icon.

▶ On the View menu at the top of the screen, select Tab Order.

▶ Click the AutoOrder button, then click OK.

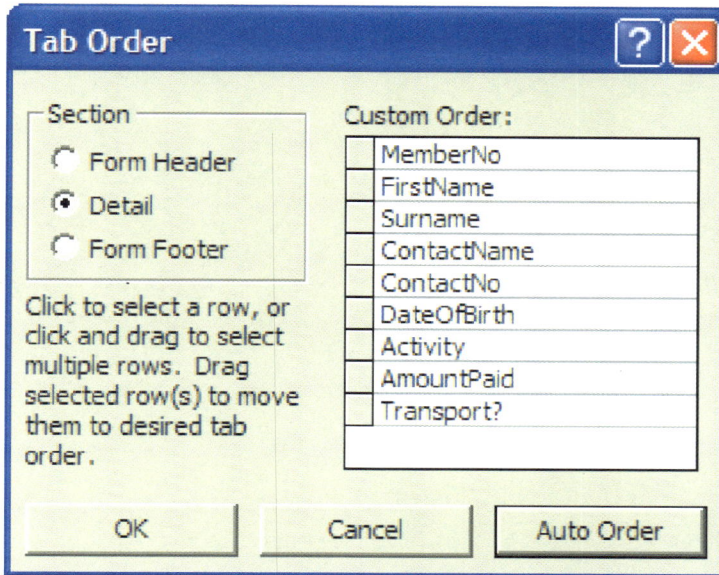

*Figure 8.11*

Return to Form View to check that the tab order is now correct.

Click in the MemberNo field at the top of the form and press either the Tab or Enter key. The cursor should visit each field in the order it appears on the form.

There's still a bit of tidying up you could do on your form. Some fields don't need to be as wide, and the labels would look better right-aligned.

Save and close the form when you are satisfied with it.

Well, that's it! Now you know the basics of Access and databases.

*Let's go dudes – we deserve a break!*

# Index